THE WINDS OF FREEDOM

The Winds of Freedom

Addressing Challenges to the University

GERHARD CASPER

Yale

UNIVERSITY PRESS

New Haven and London

Published with assistance from the Office of the
Vice President, Yale University.

Published with assistance from the foundation established in memory of
Philip Hamilton McMillan of the Class of 1894, Yale College.

Yale University Press books may be purchased in quantity for
educational, business, or promotional use. For information, please e-mail
sales.press@yale.edu (U.S. office) or sales@yaleup.co.uk (U.K. office).

Designed by Sonia Shannon.
Set in Galliard type by Westchester Book Group.
Printed in the United States of America.

Library of Congress Cataloging-in-Publication Data
Casper, Gerhard.
The winds of freedom : addressing challenges to the university / Gerhard
Casper.
     pages   cm
Includes index.
ISBN 978-0-300-19691-7 (hardback)
1. Education, Higher—Philosophy. 2. Education, Higher—Aims and
objectives. 3. Academic freedom. 4. Stanford University. I. Title.
LB2322.2.C39 2014
378.001—dc23
                                                                    2013022143

A catalogue record for this book is available from the British Library.

This paper meets the requirements of ANSI/NISO Z39.48-1992
(Permanence of Paper).

10 9 8 7 6 5 4 3 2

To Katherine and Matthew
"It is a pleasure to live . . .
Studies blossom and the minds
move."

—Ulrich von Hutten

Contents

Preface

From 1992 to 2000, I served as president of Stanford University. In those eight years, I gave, on average, about one speech every three days, not excluding weekends, holidays, or vacations. By "speech," I mean anything ranging from a formal lecture to "Pop-Up-Gerhard" remarks. ("President Casper, I am sure you would like to say a few words.") I mostly took these "speech acts" very seriously. Much of what a university president can do is accomplished with words. University governance, to a large extent, is self-governance by faculties as constituted in departments, schools, and institutes. While the president of a university has real powers and can make decisions that deeply influence the direction of the institution, much of the time he or she has to rely primarily on persuasion. Speech acts clarify what matters to the speaker and thus set a tone that is both personal and institutional.

In a 1946 letter, the University of Chicago president Robert Hutchins complained that when a university gets big and complicated, "the burden of institutional detail is so great that nobody can think of what the institution is for." My speeches—virtually all of my speeches—were an attempt to address what I think the research-intensive university is for.

They covered a wide array of topics. I wrote them mostly myself (though, of course, I benefited from some very able help), and I worried about them all the time, since, in many instances, any given occasion would be the only occasion where that particular audience was exposed to my voice as the voice of the university.

One theme that I first explored in my inaugural address may be called "freedoms of and freedoms in the university." Some of the speeches dealing with that theme are reproduced here in their unedited form. Each of the "Texts" will be followed by an afterword that I call "Context." In "Context," I discuss the circumstances amid which the speech was given. The explanations are not meant to be exhaustive but primarily aim at making the text and motivation for it more intelligible. Obviously, I represent my point of view, but I have done much archival research to gets the facts as straight as possible, always remembering that any social fact will undergo "distortions" as "it passes through value-charged fields" (Felix S. Cohen). Occasionally, I shall add observations about my "Subtext," if any, or a "Postscript" about subsequent or related matters.

My reference is not freedom in the singular, but freedoms of the students and of the faculty and also, equally important, freedoms of the university as an institution—freedoms that may be in conflict with one another. The 1990s were not marked, as were the 1960s and 1970s, by many student uprisings. Former Stanford president Richard Lyman's book about the Stanford unrest from 1966 until 1972 is called *Stanford in Turmoil.* "Turmoil" we did not experience in the 1990s, but we did encounter a range of academic freedom issues that raised core questions relevant not only to Stanford but to research-intensive universities more generally.

This is not a book about the law of academic freedom. Inescapably, law will be touched upon, but my perspective is best described as embedded in the humanities: reflections about freedoms and responsibilities at the university in a historical, philosophical, and experiential context. The book is an extended "essay in chapters." Its aim, as Felix Frankfurter once said about the essay as a literary form, is "tentative, reflective, suggestive, contradictory, and incomplete. It mirrors the perversities and complexities of life." The complexities are especially those faced by a university president. There is intentional repetitiveness, as a few of my formulations play the role of leitmotifs.

This is an idiosyncratic book. The subject seems comprehensive, but the treatment is not—far from it. The book's subject matter has many facets that I do not touch upon. Its themes were chosen only because they are general themes germane to good public and private universities, especially those of the United States, with their unique blend of undergraduate and graduate education, of teaching and research. Since in university governance both God and the devil are in the details, I engage in a fair amount of microanalysis. Therefore, the book is also a book about how I approached the responsibilities of a university president.

Some friends who read the manuscript thought that it needed biographical information beyond what is publicly available or what is mentioned in the main body of the text. Following their advice, I have reflected on several crucial experiences that helped to shape my perception of the world and present them here as a prologue.

Born in 1937, I was too young to have known the World War II period as political history. I have no personal recollections of the Nazi regime other than superficial ones. World War II, in a big city, such as my hometown Hamburg, was encountered, to some extent, as if it were an ongoing "natural" disaster with which adults and children coped as well as they could in order to survive. For the civilian targets, the experience resembled hurricanes. Indeed, the so-called Hamburg firestorm of 1943, which in four nights destroyed half the city and killed about fifty thousand people, created literally a hurricane-like effect.

In his book of essays *On the Natural History of Destruction*, W. G. Sebald gave the following description of what happened in Hamburg in 1943. On July 27

at one-twenty A.M., a firestorm of an intensity that no one would ever before have thought possible arose. The fire, now rising two thousand meters into the sky, snatched oxygen to itself so violently that the air currents reached hurricane force, resonating like mighty organs with all their stops pulled out at once. The fire burned like this for three hours. At its height, the storm . . . drove human beings before it like living torches. . . . Those who had fled from their air-raid shelters sank, with grotesque contortions in the thick bubbles thrown up by the melting asphalt. No one knows for certain how many lost their lives that night, or how many went mad before they died. When day broke, the summer dawn could not penetrate the leaden gloom above the city. The smoke had risen to a height of eight thousand meters where it spread like a vast anvil-shaped . . . cloud.

My parents, my brother, and I watched that cloud from a distance. My father's survival techniques had included listening (illegally, of course) to German-language broadcasts from London. Because of British warnings of what Air Marshall Harris had dubbed "Operation Gomorrah," our parents took my brother and me to a village thirty miles east of Hamburg before the operation began. From there, we saw the intense orange glow of "Gomorrah" burning on the horizon.

All I can remember from the war years are the air raids and a deep sense of fear and insecurity. We felt safe only when we knew that Hamburg was not a target. I shall not forget a starry summer night when we were all standing in the street while bombers were flying overhead: We were "safe" because their flight pattern and height indicated that they were headed for Lübeck, the neighboring major city to the east.

It was, of course, only years after the war that I learned about Guernica, the Basque city that the German Luftwaffe had destroyed in 1937, the year of my birth. It was only after the war that I learned about the Battle of Britain, about the Blitz, about Coventry, about the sieges of Leningrad and Stalingrad. Indeed, my *political* memories begin only in 1945, or, more precisely, on May 2, 1945, the day before the surrender of Hamburg and its occupation by the British

2nd Army on May 3. Hitler had committed suicide in Berlin on April 30; a successor government under Admiral Dönitz had been established in Flensburg.

The governor of Hamburg, Karl Kaufmann, an extreme Nazi from the first days of the party, in order to prevent "senseless, complete annihilation," surrendered the city. He announced the decision over the radio on May 2. Because of the intense emotions of relief on the part of the adults, I remember the occasion. I also remember it because in the weeks, months, years to come, the Nazi Kaufmann was given credit for not having tried what was impossible anyway—to defend Hamburg militarily, as he had been ordered to do by the Flensburg government. The British-appointed first postwar mayor, Rudolf Petersen, who came from an old Hamburg family, made use of his inaugural address on May 17, 1945, to mention that "the former holder of governmental power" had saved lives for both sides. Petersen's comments about his Nazi predecessor were published in the newspaper of the British military government.

When the Nuremberg war crimes trials were broadcast in late 1945 and 1946, I was still too young to understand their significance. At the time of the Nuremberg trials, there was, of course, no television, and thus the evidence, especially the evidence from the concentration camps, was less inescapable than television images became subsequently. Many adults thought of the trials as "victors' justice," and in this context, some mentioned the air raids that had devastated many German cities.

I was seven when the war ended. We children played among the ruins and were fed in part by American food aid, both public and private. President Truman had placed Herbert Hoover in charge of famine relief in Europe. I heard the name of the Stanford alumnus for the first time as the label attached to American food supplies that reached our schools. They were known as "Hoover foods."

Certainly neither I nor anybody else could have imagined in 1945 that one day I would become the president of Hoover's alma mater. Nor could anyone have imagined that my wife, Regina, and I would one day live in the Lou Henry Hoover House, the Hoovers' family home on the Stanford campus, which Herbert Hoover had given to the university in 1945, the year that World War II ended, to serve as the residence of the Stanford presidents.

I was educated in the postwar world. It was not an easy time to be a German: the generation of our parents contained few role models. The atrocities of the Nazis forced us to search for the reasons why and how the Germans had failed in the presence of evil. Many people thought, and many people think now, that certain aspects of the German character—that is, the character of Germans, "of ordinary men and women"—accounted for Hitler and the evil deeds of the Third Reich. In the winter of 1954, I went for the first time to the United States as the Federal Republic's delegate to an international youth forum. I had just turned sixteen. Reviewing press clippings from those days, I find myself quoted in the *New York Herald Tribune* as saying that there were times when I intensely disliked being the German representative.

Was there "collective guilt"? How was one to determine measures of individual guilt, measures of individual responsibility? The Allies' "denazification program," undertaken immediately after 1945, became a bureaucratic enterprise that many former Nazis used effectively for the purpose of having themselves classified as mere "Mitläufer," nominal hangers-on. The testimonials these followers of the Nazis solicited were known popularly, after a famous soap, as "Persilscheine," whitewash papers.

Criminal prosecutions were sporadic and not very effective in sorting out responsibility. After a slow pace at the beginning, prosecutions continued over many years, punctuated in the early decades by intermittent and laborious legislative debates about extending the regular statute of limitations for murder, whose ordinary duration would have cut off prosecutions as early as 1965.

Ordinary men and women who had been Nazis, soldiers, active participants lived among us. Some among those who had helped the Nazi onslaught on the universities were once again in their faculty positions. In the first ten years after the war, how much confrontation among citizens was bearable for a fragile population that lived among ruins faced with gigantic reconstruction tasks and, in West Germany, the additional challenge of having to absorb about eight million refugees who had been expelled from East Prussia, Pomerania, Czechoslovakia, and elsewhere? "Truth and reconciliation" commissions had not yet been invented.

I think it actually took about two decades for the enormity of the evils perpetrated during the Third Reich to sink in. It also took the tenacious work of historians who would not blink in describing the Nazi system and the atrocities committed by and in the name of Germans. Because of the initial tendency to use the label "war crimes" for description and analysis of all Nazi criminality, genocide and ethnic cleansing were not sufficiently differentiated from the war as such. It was concealing rather than clarifying, to say the least, to classify the killing of six million Jews as one item in a long list of German war deeds.

As I said, role models were few. I found some. Among them was my high school principal and history teacher, whom the Nazis had arrested in 1943 because, beginning about 1936, she had arranged to meet regularly at her home with former students for whom she provided continuing, "politically incorrect" education (among her students from that period was Helmut Schmidt, the later German chancellor). Erna Stahl–her name–was an immensely gifted pedagogue with a deep commitment to cultural history.

After her arrest by the Gestapo, Stahl was imprisoned (first in Hamburg, last in Bayreuth), suffered greatly (at one point she lost the capacity to speak), and was charged to stand trial for treason before the infamous People's Court (Volksgerichtshof). She survived because the Americans liberated her prison on April 14, 1945.

It was difficult to get Erna Stahl to talk about her personal experiences. Indeed, it was difficult to get her to talk about the Third Reich. She thought it was vastly more important to instill positive values, among them reverence for life as understood by

Albert Schweitzer. After I had graduated, my school was even renamed for Schweitzer, who visited there in 1959 and, in response to the naming of the school, captured some of what Stahl was about (I was present at the occasion): "It is encouraging to know that there are human beings who live and unswervingly fight for making the deep reverence for everything living determinant and who follow ideals that lead us beyond our own time into a new age."

Back in 1954, my eleventh-grade homeroom had had a confrontation with Stahl. It is a story about ordinary people and the Nazi past.

There was a theater in postwar Hamburg that was headed by a great actress, Ida Ehre, who was Jewish. Like Victor Klemperer, she had survived the Third Reich as the spouse of an "Aryan." My friends and I frequented her theater and greatly admired her. I can see her before my eyes now as "Mother Courage" in Brecht's famous play about the Thirty Years' War. Stahl had invited her to spend an evening at our school talking about what it meant to direct a theater.

A fellow student in my homeroom was the son of a composer who, in postwar Hamburg, was well known as the conductor of a choir. During the Third Reich, the composer had set Nazi "poetry" to music. As it turned out, his son had some neo-Nazi tendencies. The evening of Ida Ehre's visit, he donned a brownish shirt (in allusion to the Nazi storm troopers) and carried a copy of Hitler's *Mein Kampf* in his coat pocket as a form of protest. Most of us had no idea that this was happening.

When Stahl learned about the incident a couple of days later, she was beside herself and took us to task for not having squelched the matter and not having told her about it. Putting to one side the issue of informing, we countered by complaining that, by eleventh grade, we had studied ancient, medieval, and seventeenth-century political and cultural history but had yet to be taught about the Third Reich. That very morning, she canceled other classes and told us about some of her personal experiences during the Nazi period. One of them is the reason why I am recounting the story.

In 1941, Erna Stahl came down a street near where she lived when she saw that the Gestapo was loading Jews onto trucks. The victims had been told that they would be allocated a new settlement territory in the east and would be taken there by train. In reality, of course, they were shipped east to be massacred. Erna Stahl walked up to one of the guards and asked: "Where are you taking these people [diese Menschen]?" He answered: "If you want to know, get on the truck!" She then turned around and walked away.

The silence in the homeroom was complete.

In 1961, persons then thirty years or older were asked when they had first learned about the killing of the Jews: 32 percent said before the end of the war, while 58 percent said after the war. While the Nazis had engaged in concealment, reversing these percentages would seem a more plausible distribution.

Nineteen sixty-one was the year of the Eichmann trial in Jerusalem. It was a watershed event that was followed widely and that caused intense discussions for years to come, especially after the publication of Hannah Arendt's report about the trial. The pace of so-called Vergangenheitsbewältigung ("coming to terms with the past") picked up and eventually reached broad and changing audiences, especially through television.

I graduated from high school in 1957. That year, a German sociologist, Helmut Schelsky, published a book about German young people that he entitled *The Skeptical Generation* and in which he argued that my generation was distrustful of all political ideologies, ideas, and institutions, past and present. A profound sense of insecurity and disillusionment had led us, Schelsky said, to focus on our own lives and on our families rather than public life. "Ohne mich"—"without me"—was the slogan that supposedly characterized the skeptical generation.

A highly developed skepticism was not just a German phenomenon. In England in the 1950s, an antiestablishment group of writers emerged: the "angry young men," of whom John Osborne was the best known. When I was a student at the University of

Freiburg, a Swiss fellow student, who to me represented a background of traditions, stability, and normalcy that I had never known, made fun of me, implying that I should have been a charter member of the "angry young men."

My speech as high school valedictorian in 1957 dealt doubtfully with the topic of role models but, Schelsky to the contrary, suggested nowhere that my graduating class felt disengaged. I quoted a poem by Wolfgang Borchert, a Hamburg poet who was much beloved by my classmates and me: "I should like to be a lighthouse, in the night and in the wind, for cod and for smelt, for every boat, but, alas, I myself am no more than a ship in distress." I went on to say that in our search for role models we would be looking not for "lighthouses" but for "beach fires" that—while exposed to the elements, just as we were—continued to burn nevertheless. The metaphor was heartfelt, though, upon rereading it, I am not sure I understand it completely. It gave me some anonymous fame, however, since a prominent theologian at the University of Hamburg, Helmut Thielicke, whom I had come to know, quoted the valedictory at some length in one of his books as an example of the "de-Platonization" of ideals.

Following the European pattern, upon graduating from high school, I enrolled at the university, specializing immediately. I had chosen law because I thought I might enter the foreign service as a career, and legal studies were considered useful for that purpose. In the German fashion—you could then change universities at will—I started out at the University of Hamburg but moved on to the University of Freiburg in my second year, later returned to Hamburg, and ultimately went again to Freiburg for my doctorate, with the legal philosopher Erik Wolf as my adviser.

During my first stay at Freiburg, as a third-semester student, I went to Konrad Hesse, a well-known professor of constitutional law, and asked to be admitted to his advanced seminar. He thought that could not be done, but eventually yielded and assigned me a paper on the subject of judicial review. Hesse's seminar had a profound impact on my future. It taught me the value of small-group interactions (normal law courses in German universities had hundreds of registrants). It taught me that even a beginner could benefit and could contribute. It kindled my interest in constitutional law. And, finally, it made me desire an academic career.

The sine qua non for becoming an academic in the United States, rather than in Germany, was the year I spent as a graduate student at the Yale Law School. I had applied to attend Yale, upon the completion of my law studies in Hamburg, because of an interest in the work of Harold Lasswell, one of the leading behavioral political scientists of the twentieth century, who was on the faculty of the law school and there, jointly with law colleague Myres McDougal, taught a course called "Law, Science, and Policy." The "policy" part of the course put forward a systematic "value-oriented jurisprudence" that claimed to be empirically based. While Lasswell was actually away from Yale during the 1961–62 academic year, I took "Law, Science, and Policy" from "Mac" (as he was known to the students) and, throughout the year, displayed considerable skepticism about the Lasswell-McDougal approach. At the end of the course, McDougal, a prodigious and extraordinarily courtly Mississippian, called me to his office and said something to the effect that he understood that I disagreed with him a lot but that he thought well of me and if I wanted a teaching position in the United States he would help me to find one. I cannot say that McDougal had singled me out from all the other graduate students; rather, he viewed placement as an obligation and an opportunity.

The year I spent at Yale was extraordinary. It not only strengthened my interest in constitutional law under the influence of faculty that included Charles Black, Alexander Bickel, and Fred Rodell but also exposed me to ways of thinking I had not previously encountered, in seminars with F. S. C. Northrop, Joseph Goldstein, and Jay Katz. "Stimulating" is the appropriate adjective to characterize the environment for research, discourse, and intellectual openness at the law school. Furthermore, it would then have been hard to conceive of many places in Europe where a professor with whom you had had mostly disputes would take the initiative to recommend you for a faculty position.

Due to McDougal's efforts on my behalf I was, in 1964, recruited as an assistant professor of political science to the University of California at Berkeley. The subjects I was to cover were comparative law and legal theory. Beginning in 1965, I also taught at the law school. The Political Science Department at the time was deeply split into a normative theory faction and a behaviorist one. This split had political consequences since the normative group, in the context of the university's then intense politics, tended to be "liberal," while many of the behaviorists were more oriented toward support of the university establishment. (This had little to do with epistemological and methodological differences, as I learned when I went to Chicago, where the Political Science Department was similarly split but the political implications were the opposite from those at Berkeley.)

At the end of 1964, I married Regina Koschel. Regina and I had met in 1963 at the University of Freiburg, where she was doing research for her doctoral thesis in the school of medicine and I was writing my dissertation on American legal realism. Following our wedding in New York City (at the Upper West Side apartment of Charlotte Beradt, a refugee from Nazi Germany whom I had met through Erna Stahl), we united in California. Our two years in Berkeley were years of forming friendships with Berkeley colleagues and of acculturation to an American campus of the greatest quality in deep crisis—an experience that made me reflect for the first time about some of the issues that I address in this book. However, when, in 1966, I was made an offer by the law school of the University of Chicago, both of us decided, for professional reasons, to leave California. The politicization of the campus did not help to keep us there.

We spent the next twenty-six years happily in Chicago, Regina at Michael Reese Hospital, as a professor of psychiatry at the University of Illinois and then at the University of Chicago; I as a professor of law (with a joint appointment in political science for half the time), as dean of the law school (for nine years), and, appointed by Hanna Gray in 1989, as provost of the university (for three years). Of all major American universities, the University of Chicago was probably the one most emphatically committed to "the life of the mind." Pieties, fads, and fashions were persistently questioned. I learned much from colleagues and students, and scholarly discussions were many, intense, and, for the most part, "uninhibited, robust, and wide-open" (to use one of my favorite mantras from a 1964 opinion of Supreme Court Justice William Brennan).

There were too many influences and friends to acknowledge even a discrete number of them. I shall, however, mention Phil Neal, who was the dean who recruited me and became a role model for my own service as dean; my constitutional law colleague and the wise counselor and friend of all my Chicago years, Philip Kurland; and, finally the person Phil Neal assigned me to teach a seminar with during my first quarter at the law school: Edward Levi, former law school dean, provost when I first met him, and subsequently president of the university. (In 1975 President Ford appointed him attorney general.) I was deeply influenced by him, as I will readily acknowledge throughout this book, and, of course, followed in his steps when I became dean of the law school, then provost at Chicago, and finally president, but that at Stanford.

The book's focus is on only a very few selected aspects of what I tried to accomplish as the Stanford president. While it is highly Stanford-centric, I hope the reader understands that what I say is meant to have implications for all research-intensive universities that still take themselves seriously as universities.

Since this book has a theme, it will not address a large number of subjects that I focused on as president. There is no chapter on the reforms in undergraduate education that we undertook, there is no chapter on the resolution of the preexisting dispute with the federal government about alleged overcharges for overhead, there is no chapter on reorganizations, no chapter on our first experiments with online education, there is no chapter on the medical center, no chapter on architecture, no chapter on development and fundraising. Some of these matters were dealt with in a report I wrote that is entitled *Cares of the University*. It was published in 1997 by the Office of the President and is readily available on the web.

However, I should devote a few lines to educational reforms because of their relevance to many aspects of this book. At the end of my first year at Stanford, I appointed a Commission on Undergraduate Education. It was chaired by the historian James Sheehan. The commission made its report in 1994, and the faculty senate acted quickly and decisively to accept most of its recommendations.

The report said about the aims of education: "The university should encourage many qualities of mind and spirit—a potential for leadership, a devotion to public service, an appreciation of beauty— but its special mission, and its distinctive contribution to the well-being of society, is to demonstrate the value of free inquiry and tolerant debate by engaging its students in the search for knowledge."

Among the outcomes of our reforms, accomplished by 1997, were Introductory Seminars for Freshmen and Sophomores (limited to twelve to sixteen students, about two hundred such seminars are now taught every year by regular Stanford faculty), Sophomore College (admitted students take a single class limited to fourteen students for three weeks, five days a week, before the beginning of their second year), a substantial increase in undergraduate research opportunities, and an Honors College in the summer before the senior year. In 2012, the university conducted a detailed review of the effectiveness of these programs and found them to have clearly achieved their goal of providing students with serious academic opportunities in a research-intensive university.

In my 1996 remarks to the faculty senate, in which I called for the Introductory Seminars, I also said we would raise an endowment for graduate fellowships in those areas where we relied heavily on federal research grants for graduate student support. I was greatly concerned about the fragility of federal research programs and wanted to enable the university and its faculty to compete for the best graduate students. The Stanford Graduate Fellowships Program also was begun in 1997. In strengthening the opportunities for both undergraduate and graduate students, my overriding purpose was to "secure the unique synthesis of teachers and students that marks the true university."

After I stepped down as president on August 31, 2000, I applied myself to the "synthesis of teachers and students" by teaching freshmen in their first quarter as part of an Introduction to the Humanities requirement the university then maintained. I also taught in Sophomore College and at the law school. I headed the executive committee of Stanford's Arts Initiative, a transformative effort to strengthen the role of the arts at the university. Now formally an emeritus professor, I still maintain an active involvement in the university as a Senior Fellow at Stanford's Freeman Spogli Institute for International Studies, where I served as interim director during the academic year 2012–13.

THE WINDS OF FREEDOM

1.

Roles of a
University President

The appointment as president of a major research-intensive university does not come with a clear and concise job description. Therefore, let me provide background and introduction by talking about how I viewed and experienced what can be characterized as at least nine jobs.

1. *College president.* When I was recruited as president of Stanford, I did not realize that the most visible job I was taking on was a job that almost everybody in the country referred to as "college" president. The designation "college" president suggests a nineteenth-century image of somebody who walks around a small campus in a tweed jacket with leather patches on his elbows to chat with faculty and students and admire the fall colors. And, indeed, there were quite a few people who thought the only thing I did in the summer was to get ready for the first football game of the fall. When I read in the newspapers that I was a "college" president, I was reminded of the image conjured up by Daniel Webster in the oral argument of the Dartmouth College case: "Yes, sir, a small college and yet there are those who love it."

It is true that, as far as public attention is concerned, the focus is mostly on the undergraduate side of universities. The "college" aspect of a university president's job makes itself especially felt with

1

respect to most "hot button" issues involving undergraduate education, such as admissions, curriculum, tuition costs, and athletics.

The undergraduate experience in the United States, and in the United States only, significantly includes college athletics, especially football and basketball. For the president this may involve such high-visibility issues as who will be the football coach, and on what terms, or worrying about the so-called friendly rivalry between competing athletic teams that so easily can turn distinctly hostile.

When I first arrived at Stanford, I was somewhat infamous for—perish the thought—not caring about football. After all, I came to Stanford from the University of Chicago, which is known as a *former* member of the Big Ten. I was quickly taught a lesson about the significance of football. When the time came to pick the one person who had the greatest impact on Stanford in the first year of its second century, the student newspaper chose Bill Walsh, who, at about the same time I had been chosen as president, had returned to Stanford as the football coach. "Bill Walsh has had more of an invigorating effect on campus than the university president," June Cohen, the *Stanford Daily* editor, told the *New York Times*. "Casper hasn't come out with anything that's gotten people real riled up or real excited," she continued.

Time demands of the athletic enterprise can be quite significant and include attendance at games, but also issues involving compliance with one of the most elaborate, micromanaging regulatory entities ever designed: the National Collegiate Athletic Association (NCAA). The pinnacle of my career in public life probably was a position I held (on account of seniority) for the last two years of my presidency: the chairmanship of the then-Pacific-10 athletic conference. My first meeting as chair dealt with the question of whether the Pac-10 should employ baseball bats made of wood or of aluminum.

To most people, outside and *inside* the university, the president is an abstraction: the responsibilities of the office are ill-understood, the person occupying the office seems distant to most. Frequently, one becomes a figment of the imagination of journalists (both the professional and student variety). If the president is a recruit from outside the university, as I was, there will be a fair amount of distrust of his or her grasp of the "true" nature of the particular institution that has become his charge. Does he really understand "what Stanford is all about"?

In the case of Stanford, major regional newspapers still maintained a regular Stanford beat (and national and foreign media paid a lot of attention). Under these circumstances, one could not help but be concerned about how motives and purposes get attributed in and by the press and how statements come to be overinterpreted (and silences misconstrued). Harold Shapiro, president first of Michigan and then of Princeton, discontinued reading campus and local papers upon becoming president because he did not, he said, want others to set his agenda. While this abstinence served President Shapiro well (he was a great president), I decided I better read the papers in order to find out what I had supposedly done the day before so that I could set my own agenda all the more clearly.

In a *Wall Street Journal* editorial many years ago, Albert R. Hunt had this to say about "college presidents": "Few callings face such demanding and compelling claims from constituencies with so little in common—students, faculty, alumni, contributors, athletic boosters, local communities." Hunt barely scratched the surface. First of all, his list of "constituencies" can be extended to state and federal governments, businesses and unions, religious organizations, even foreign countries. When the Stanford Band, known—in its own words—for "loud music and burning political satire," overreached at a football game against Notre Dame (did the members of the band have free speech rights?), I heard from the Trustees of Notre Dame (they demanded that I apologize, which I did), the San Jose diocese, the Ancient Order of Hibernia, the United Irish Organizations of Nebraska, and newspapers in the Republic of Ireland.

More to the point, the categories Hunt mentions are themselves divided and subdivided into myriad interest groups. I sometimes said at alumni meetings that I would drown in contradictions if I attempted to reconcile all the advice I received from alumni about curriculum, student and faculty rights and obligations, campus architecture, university investments, or what the university's priorities should be. Hunt said the claims of these (often self-appointed) constituencies are demanding and compelling. They are certainly, much of the time, demanding.

Land use provides a prime example. Leland and Jane Stanford's eight thousand–acre stock farm near Palo Alto became the university's campus (therefore Stanford's nickname, "The Farm"). The university has developed about one-third of its lands. Much of the "green foothills" of the Santa Cruz Mountains constitute the so-called academic reserve. Some would like to bar the university from ever building there. Let me quote from a missive concerning the foothills. It came from a group calling itself, among other things, "a network of students, faculty, staff and alumni": "As alumni, we have special standing and special power to influence Stanford's decisions. . . . To a great degree, we are the University, and the University is ours." Who, you might ask, empowered these particular individuals to speak for the university or, for that matter, for present and future Stanford students, for Stanford alumni in the Bay Area, Chicago, Los Angeles, or New York City, not to forget those in Hong Kong and London, and not to mention the Board of Trustees and its special fiduciary duties under Leland and Jane Stanford's founding grant?

2. *University president.* Even more than a "college president," I was a university president with responsibility for teaching and research, academic clinical care, and a dizzying number of "product lines." The university president serves as the chief executive officer of a major corporation with a budget that, in the case of Stanford, exceeds the budgets of many countries in the world. In my years as president, faculty numbered almost seventeen hundred, students in excess of fourteen thousand, and staff, in the university proper, nine thousand. All of these categories have grown in size since then.

More than half of Stanford's students are enrolled in graduate and professional programs. In addition to the Ph.D. programs in the School of Humanities and Sciences, doctorates can be earned in all six other schools. Graduate education also leads to professional degrees in law, business, education, medicine, and engineering. Research funded by outside sources, mostly the federal government, constitutes about 30 percent of the university budget. There are research centers and institutes, including the SLAC National Accelerator Laboratory, a federal facility on Stanford land that is operated by the university under contract with the Department of Energy. The university owns two hospitals.

A university president is a CEO under very special conditions. Under normal circumstances, a business CEO has both fairly far-reaching policy-making and executive powers, a university president not much of either. In the contemporary university (as distinguished from earlier times), the president is an authority with limited direct power who, nevertheless, is accountable or held to be accountable for virtually all activities of and *in* the institution.

A faculty member once sent me (for "the humility section" of my quotations file) the following item: "When [then] Harvard professor of government James Q. Wilson was informed that his name was on a list of those being considered for a university presidency, Wilson wrote to Harvard colleague Harvey Mansfield that he was not interested in being president of anything. Mansfield is said to have written back: 'You're probably wise not to be interested in a presidency. The job is more difficult than important.' "

Students, if they bother to consider the subject at all (which the majority wisely don't), think of the president as a fairly obscure celebrity of some kind, or as a service provider known as "the administration." Some suspect that the president is part of, or at least in bed with, the hegemonic establishment. Some, whose parents pay full tuition (a minority) and who have an exaggerated notion of what proportion of expenditures per student are paid for by tuition, believe the president is, as an undergraduate solemnly advised me, their "employee." With a lot of effort, the president may succeed in becoming a human presence on campus to whom the students relate as a person. In my case, that took at least two to three years.

Sometimes there is not even a hope of success. A friend of mine on the Harvard faculty once mentioned the name of Drew Faust (the current Harvard president) to his granddaughter, a student at Harvard and the offspring of two Harvard alumni: "She asked who Drew Faust was and I answered, 'the president'; whereupon she said to me: 'I didn't know Harvard had a president.'"

Given the considerable ambiguities and uncertainties concerning the president's role, I was taken aback when I read the prospectus for the first Stanford bond offering during my presidency. It said: "The Founding Grant provides that the Board shall appoint the President of the University. The President prescribes the duties of professors and teachers, sets the course of study and the mode and manner of teaching, and exercises all other necessary powers relating to the educational, financial and business affairs of the University. The President appoints, subject to confirmation by the Board, the senior officers of the University, except that the President of Stanford Management Company is appointed by the Board of Directors with the concurrence of the President."

As to the first point, all I can say is "Dream on!" Concerning the areas of greatest importance at a university—faculty appointments, admissions, and curriculum—all the real power necessarily is from bottom up.

If the last sentence of the quotation suggests that my responsibilities as to the investment policies of the Stanford Management Company were somewhat attenuated, a rude awakening came in the first few months of my tenure, when the university's outside auditors advised me that I was responsible for the performance of Stanford Management Company since, legally, it was nothing other than an administrative unit of the university, not a separate corporation.

Given that, to a large extent, faculty and students are and act as independent agents, the notion of independence is popular with some university staff as well. When the provost, Condoleezza Rice, and I appointed a new director of an administrative department early in my tenure, a decision that had important policy implications, the comment in a staff meeting was: "Well, I hope she [the new director] understands that she is not working for the president and provost."

Under conditions that occasionally look like structured anarchy, as the CEO of a major corporation, the university president is nevertheless responsible for compliance with laws, regulations, and rules that apply generally to individuals and business corporations and then with those that specifically address higher education. Not a year goes by when the federal government (which has no substantive jurisdiction over higher education to begin with) does not pass several laws or regulations to attend to some perceived or real shortcoming of colleges and universities. I estimate, conservatively I should stress, that at least fifteen cents of every tuition dollar goes to unreimbursed regulatory compliance costs.

Stating the situation abstractly does not give the full flavor. Let me list the *major* legal issues that I had to deal with over eight years:

- federal government indirect cost rules (that is, the charges for overhead at the university and medical center);
- state environmental protection regulations intended for refineries and other industrial producers but applied equally to student chemistry experiments;
- Medicare and Medicaid reimbursement regulations;
- coding of health care procedures for purposes of reimbursement (with large financial and reputational costs attached to possible errors);
- federal civil rights statutes (including such matters as the prohibition of gender discrimination in athletics programs);
- federal affirmative action regulations;
- state civil rights legislation;

- contract disputes with the Department of Energy about the Linear Accelerator Center;
- local government and land use laws running the gamut from campus traffic and density of development to size of buildings and use of trails in Stanford's foothills;
- employment litigation, with 150 or so cases pending at any given time, almost all involving disputes between staff employees and their supervisors, including alleged wrongful termination, sexual harassment, OSHA investigations, and similar matters;
- faculty grievances and faculty discipline.

There are general laws, such as those prohibiting drinking by those under age twenty-one, that pose particular enforcement challenges in a university environment: Attempting to deal with them conscientiously without creating a police state atmosphere presents extraordinary difficulties in a population of young people who have just come of age and who, for the first time away from home, are out "to find themselves."

3. *Trustee.* The third job of a university president is being a trustee of a trust established in perpetuity. A university president is in fact the leading fiduciary for his or her institution; he or she must maintain what is excellent and, simultaneously, be a change agent. One has fiduciary duties not only for the present but also for the future in a setting in which some incumbent faculty and students find it hard to understand why the university does not devote its resources primarily to the present generation, given that generation's many excellences, legitimate claims, and clearly articulated preferences.

The fiduciary duties are manifold. Important among them are maintenance of the endowment and of the physical plant. These two can be in conflict with each other, and trade-offs can be badly miscalculated if, for instance, holding down endowment payout leads to substantial deferred maintenance bills for a rapidly deteriorating building stock.

Fiduciary duties include—at least to my mind—campus architecture, given its lasting impact. The world often forgets that the visual art we are most exposed to on a daily basis is architecture: architecture pure and simple and architecture in its sculptural potential. It has the wonderful, but also frequently distressing, quality of being inescapable. This is why, to me, competitive architectural design is so important in the exercise of good stewardship at our universities—maintaining the physical endowment that has been handed down to us and, then, renewing it as needed to meet the changing nature of teaching, learning, and research, but also aesthetics.

Among the fiduciary duties is concern for the reputation of the institution. I mention it because the task is quite demanding in light of myriad voices on campus, each of which believes that its cause trumps all institutional causes and that it must speak and be heard even if, in consequence, the institution might suffer severe damage. When a university president raises a cautionary note about the "free-for-alls," he or she will frequently be accused of being an autocrat or worse.

Occupying an important place among fiduciary obligations is fund-raising and alumni relations. The thought and effort that go into these activities justify their characterization as a separate, fourth job category.

4. *Fiduciary for alumni relations and for fund-raising.* The time that is spent on alumni relations, development, and fund-raising is a substantial, though uncertain, portion of a president's work. I say "uncertain" because so much of everything else one does has some bearing on development. When, following Stanford's centennial campaign (which had just ended upon my arrival at Stanford as the first $1 billion campaign of any American university), the very able vice president for development, John Ford, was worried about the future of fund-raising at Stanford and wanted significant time allocations from me for direct fund-raising, I pointed out that first we had to attend to the academic priorities of the university so that

we would have clearly defined goals. Subsequently, I engaged in what I thought of as "project-oriented," albeit highly visible and campaignlike, fundraising.

It is fascinating how many faculty and students seem to assume (wrongly) that fund-raising is what the president does 90 percent of his time. Some, occasionally, turn their assumption into accusations about the president's motives in relation to all other responsibilities. ("He is raising money from alumni," as one student said about me in the *Stanford Daily*.)

Alumni relations are by no means exclusively devoted to fundraising, nor should they be. When I became president, the Stanford alumni association was an independent organization. I spent much time in a successful effort to integrate the association into the university. Without that integration, I found it difficult to fulfill the president's fiduciary duties in relation to alumni.

5. *Educator.* A fifth role of the university president is to be an educator. One must attempt to educate students, faculty, staff, alumni, parents, and "the public" about what needs to be the focus (that is, teaching, learning, and research rather than being all things to all people), what needs to change, what needs to be preserved, and, perhaps most important, what must *not* be done.

One of the great university presidents of the past fifty years, Edward Levi, led by educating. His speeches were part of an educational effort to counter the confusion, carelessness, and folly, which, he wearily saw, too often ambushed the educational enterprise.

Levi led by never misleading about the bedrock principles of the university to which he was utterly committed. Against those who seek to use universities for political and social purposes, he dared to say that "the object of the University is intellectual, not moral." Of course, for Edward Levi, adherence to reason partook of the highest morality. "Education, when it is at its best," he said, "is both a disruptive and fulfilling process. The question-asking is never ended. We pretend, at least, to welcome these questions." The irony is classic Levi.

The university president's educational task alone is extraordinarily demanding. As I indicated in the preface, in my eight years, I gave roughly one thousand speeches. I once found myself delivering twelve speeches on twelve subject matters over a forty-eight-hour period: one speech every four hours, and I was not running for political office. In reality, of course, a university president is "running for office" on a daily basis, because one cannot do one's job without having adequate support for trying to accomplish what needs to be done.

Since there is so little time for reflection, reading, or discussion, one has to start out with considerable intellectual capital that one can subsequently draw upon. I use this metaphor advisedly because there were times when I felt I did not have a single penny left in the bank.

6. *Scholar in university service.* Sixth, the president of a major research-intensive university also needs to be what the Stanford historian David Kennedy has called "a scholar in university service."

I strongly believe that the fashionable inclination to stress managerial business skills in lieu of a university president's academic background is, most of the time, ill advised. The former are clearly needed, but the latter is also indispensable. Since so much depends on the academic direction of the university, a president needs to be accepted as one of the faculty. At Stanford Faculty Senate meetings, president and provost sit among the faculty in their alphabetically determined seats, not at some podium in the front. They speak when called upon. They are "of" the faculty. One also needs to continue to have a hand in teaching and, ideally, in research. I was able to underscore my views about the changes Stanford should make (and did indeed make) in undergraduate education by teaching undergraduate seminars. I even published a book about the constitutional separation of powers (two books, if one counts *Cares of the University*).

7. *Public figure.* Job no. 7 is being a public figure: on campus, in a region, in a state. In the case of some universities, such as Stanford, the president is also a national figure, and indeed a figure

worldwide. When I spoke at the centenary of Peking University, media in the People's Republic of China, Hong Kong, and Taiwan all seemed equally interested in my presence and in the substance of my remarks.

At times, the public figure ends up being a celebrity, with all the emptiness that that status conveys. Once, along with other university presidents, I attended a meeting at the White House with the president and the vice president of the United States. As I emerged from the gathering at the Pennsylvania Avenue exit, a group of eleven- and twelve-year-old school children insisted on shaking my hand. I said to them: "But you don't know who I am!" To which I received the prompt response: "Oh, that doesn't matter."

A 1998 survey of Stanford alumni showed that, after six years, 77 percent could name me as the president of the university. It also showed that personal appearances have a measurable impact on the alumni's views of the president. In eight years, I was exposed to hundreds of thousands of people: at Stanford, around the country, and around the world. In addition to events that involved speaking to and with groups large and small, these encounters ranged from meetings with impoverished parents from the Central Valley of California to helping in the recruitment of an Italian Virgil scholar to hosting a luncheon for the emperor and empress of Japan. Most of the time, the first impression is the only impression people will have of the incumbent president of a university and thus much rides on it for the institution. Given that a university president is a fiduciary, the manner in which one relates to various publics is of real consequence.

The public figure status leads to demands on university presidents to take positions on public issues. Many of my fellow university presidents and I deferred from speaking out on any and every societal issue that might come before us, with the result that some outsiders labeled us as a "cowardly" generation of "college presidents," especially as compared to an age when giants, such as Robert Maynard Hutchins, strode the earth. Hutchins, the famous president of the University of Chicago who, among other things, opposed American entry into World War II, and other presidents, before and since, in my judgment, have caused a fair amount of harm by encouraging the expectation that this is what university presidents should do.

I was infamous for being especially austere when it came to politics. Other than on issues directly pertaining to the university or higher education, I do not believe I had a brief to commit the university politically—and, let us face it, my views or support were solicited primarily because of the university whose president I was and not because of my personal reputation. Put differently, I did not believe that *my* free speech right gave me a license publicly to address any and all issues that caught my fancy, and to do so by nature of my position as the representative head of Stanford.

Beginning with my inaugural address, I quoted, over and over again, the Report on the University's Role in Political and Social Action that a committee, chaired by a former law school colleague of mine, Harry Kalven, issued at the University of Chicago in 1967. It focused on the fact that a university cannot reach a collective position on the issues of the day without inhibiting that full freedom of dissent on which it thrives.

Fiduciary duties aside, I also found myself in the position of John Steinbeck, who, in a 1939 letter to his uncle, wrote about the many requests he received to be an espouser, to be a voice: "I don't *know* enough to pontificate."

8. *Social worker.* The university president is also a social worker. Many people entertain the view that the president should solve their problems by intervening in individual cases, whether it be a matter of unpaid student fees, a legacy admission, a salary perceived as too low, a family tragedy, or parking. The demands can be many on the service provider that the modern university has become. Clark Kerr, the distinguished former president of the University of California,

once said that a university president's job was to provide parking for the faculty, sex for the students, and football for the alumni. Given the need to figure out what to do about faculty members' "significant others," and as the president of a university that had to ban freshmen from bringing cars to campus, I think Clark Kerr's formulation may have to be changed, so that the job of a modern-day university president is to supply sex for the faculty and parking for the students. For the alumni, football still figures high.

9. *Entertainer.* Finally, job no. 9 is "entertainer." Saul Bellow opens his novel *Ravelstein* with the declaration: "Anyone who wants to govern the country has to entertain it." That insight also is applicable to university presidents. One year, just before Christmas, the following appearances were on my schedule over a three-week period. Week 1: At a charity dinner for the benefit of our hospital that was occasioned by the opening of a Bloomingdale's at the Stanford Shopping Center, I warmed up the audience for Liza Minnelli. Week 2: I amused a full house of students three nights in a row (add one night for rehearsal) by playing myself and also performing the Macarena at the so-called Big Game Gaieties—an annual student variety show calling for annual presidential participation. Week 3: I read a Christmas story at a dorm while the faculty resident fellow served potato latkes with applesauce in honor of Chanukah.

The life of a modern university president is very unlike the contemplative life of an abbot, or, for that matter, the mode of existence of past university presidents. The Yale alumni magazine, some years ago, carried an article contrasting the calendar of Whit Griswold, president of Yale from 1951 to 1963, to that of Benno Schmidt, president from 1986 to 1992. President Griswold had "one appointment in the morning and one in the afternoon" while Schmidt's calendar typically contained appointments from 7 A.M. to 11 P.M. The presidency, I quote, "which once allowed time for scholarship, teaching, and writing and socializing with faculty and students, has not only grown more time-consuming, it has become vastly more complex."

Cartoonist Scott Willis of the *San Jose Mercury News* nicely captured this complexity in March 1992. His cartoon purported to be page 1 of 100 of the application form for president of San Jose State University. The box for "ethnicity" had such hyphenated categories as "Euro-American," "Native-American," "African-American," "Japanese-American," and the like, and instructed the applicant to "check as many as possible." The religion box mentioned "Atheist," "Buddhist," "Catholic," "Protestant," "Jewish," "Hindu," "Satanic," "Other," and "Football." You were to "check all applicable." As to football specifically, it gave three choices: "I love it," "I love it," and "I love it." The questionnaire contained six categories for "sexual orientation" as well as asking the applicant: "Are you politically: correct, incorrect, confused?"

The point of the cartoon is obviously that a president is supposed to be all things to all people. That is also the view of many letters, editorials, and other communications that inform the university president that the author is "appalled," "totally shocked," "dismayed," "scandalized," "deeply saddened," "nauseated," "sick to his stomach," or "disgusted" by something the president, or somebody else at the university, is perceived to have done or failed to do. In developing skin thick enough to shrug it all off, one risks becoming callous. At times, though, the hyperbole can be quite entertaining. My favorite example had to do with long-range plans of the university to move the first hole of the Stanford Golf Course to make room for faculty housing (an urgent need). A lawyer from southern California informed me (it was not tongue-in-cheek): "To do so would be an outrageous abomination akin to disturbing sacred burial grounds."

The person who takes on a university presidency must be modest enough to realize that, in the end, he or she will have presided over just another transition period in the institution's history. When I announced that I would step down after eight years, John Ross, a Stanford chemist and winner of the National Medal of Science, wrote me, quoting Goethe: "In reality this kind of work is never finished. One has to declare it finished when, in accord with time and circumstances, one has done the utmost."

While there may be few jobs in American public life that are more challenging, there also are few that are more mind-stretching and satisfying—and: *one can make a difference.* At least that is what I tried to do.

2.

The Wind of Freedom Blows

Inaugural Address, Frost Amphitheater

OCTOBER 2, 1992

Text

Fellow members of the first-year class and fellow transfer students; Mr. Freidenrich and members of the Board of Trustees; Presidents Emeriti Kennedy and Lyman; my colleagues on the faculty and staff; Stanford students, alumni, and friends; ladies and gentlemen:

On March 17, when I first arrived on the Farm in my new role as president-elect, I was put to what you might call an "advanced placement test." I flunked it—as my fellow first-year students will be reassured, if not delighted, to learn. I had dinner with a group of excellent people to discuss the following day's news conference when Professor Sheehan, of the History Department, innocently—or not so innocently—asked me whether I knew Stanford's motto. I had no choice but to admit my ignorance.

The next day—having spent the intervening hours educating myself—I was able to remind everyone else that Stanford's first president, David Starr Jordan, chose *Die Luft der Freiheit weht* ("The wind of freedom blows") as the informal motto. It still can be found in the president's seal, which adorns the front cover of your printed program. It is obvious—at least it is obvious to me—that Jordan put it there in German, rather than in English, in order to enable me to speculate, at my first press conference, that the trustees had chosen me because they wanted a president who could pronounce the original properly.

Alas, I have bad news for the Board of Trustees. Historical research shows that the original of the original is in Latin and reads *videtis illam spirare libertatis auram.* Since it is notorious that no two students of Latin the world over can agree on its pronunciation, there is no particular reason why my pronunciation should be preferred. If, under these circumstances, the trustees would feel it appropriate to renounce their contract with me, I would understand perfectly. All I ask for is the opportunity to finish this speech.

However, in case the trustees would rather not start the presidential search all over, I now formally and with a strong sense of my own shortcomings accept the responsibility Stanford University has seen fit to confer upon me. After Canadian-born Wally Sterling, I shall be the second Stanford president of foreign origin—though I wager the English taught me by Frau Beza in Hamburg is more distinct than the English Wally Sterling learned growing up in Ontario.

Permit me to quote at the outset from the opening of Sterling's own remarks at *his* inauguration in 1949 and to adopt his words as expressing my own sentiments at this occasion. Sterling said:

> I accept this responsibility with pride. I am proud to be one of that noble company of men and women whose business is education, and I am proud to be associated with this University.
>
> I accept my responsibilities with humility. . . . I have read something of Stanford's history. It has not been untroubled by adversities and disappointments. But it is essentially the story of strong growth from good soil and, as any person is enhumbled in the presence of

greatness, so I am in the knowledge of what has been accomplished here.

Stanford University is a wondrously varied institution: rich in talent and educational opportunities; rich in research and scholarship; rich in athletic challenges; rich in artistic creativity; rich in loyalty of alumni and friends; rich in past and present contributions to California, the nation, and the world. As measured in terms of what Stanford should contribute to the future, it may not be rich in financial resources, but it is rich in its capacity as a university to pull together and to do its work, the work of a university—the work of a *great* university—with integrity and determination.

The true university, however old, must draw together and reinvent itself every day. To put it differently and to exaggerate only slightly, even after one hundred years—or, for that matter, five hundred years—the days of a university are always *first* days. The work of the university is work that cannot be done unless it is continuously reconsidered and supported afresh and jointly by faculty, students, staff, and, last but not least, by alumni and friends. I am looking forward with much hope and much confidence to our years of "first days" in common at Stanford.

I should like to return to the motto. David Starr Jordan's choice of *Die Luft der Freiheit weht* shows a high degree of learnedness on his part. By scientific discipline he was a biologist. I am, of course, not suggesting that I find this degree of learnedness surprising in a biologist. Perish the thought. However, Jordan was famous—not to say infamous—for his preoccupation with his field of specialization, ichthyology, the study of fishes.

When the bacteriologist Zinsser, in 1910, took up an appointment at Stanford, he was given advice on how to get along with President Jordan. I quote:

> If you wish to be a success at Stanford, work on fish. Jordan himself, when he works at all, works on fish. . . . The physiologist . . . works on fish. . . . The geologists,

the paleontologists, the botanists, the English Department, the Romance Languages, even the philosophers—they all work on fish. Go there, my boy, be happy, and work on fish.

How did we get a motto that nowhere mentions fish? The just-quoted calumny notwithstanding, David Starr Jordan had the most wide-ranging interests. Among these was the German humanist Ulrich von Hutten, who had lived from 1488 until 1523, and who, in the course of the nineteenth century, had captured the public imagination as an early fighter for secular freedom. The famous theologian David Friedrich Strauss had published a two-volume biography of Hutten that Jordan had read in the German original and on which he based his own sketch of Hutten's life, first published in 1886. It is in Strauss's biography that we find the German version of Hutten's Latin text that Jordan, after suggesting it to Mr. Stanford, got accepted as the unofficial Stanford motto. In Jordan's words: "Mr. Stanford was impressed with the winds of freedom—which we hoped would continue to blow over Stanford University."

As I have mentioned, Hutten was born in 1488. He belonged to the lesser German nobility that at the time found itself severely squeezed by the princes of the Holy Roman Empire and by the church. On account of his weak constitution, young Hutten was sent to a monastery school for a career in the church. However, at age seventeen, the age of some of you in the audience this morning, he fled the monastery and became a vagrant student, moving from one university to another in search of humanistic learning, first in Germany, then in Italy. He had greater difficulties in finding the right place than you have had in settling on Stanford.

Hutten's earliest claim to fame is his role in a celebrated controversy concerning the preservation of Hebrew literature against efforts to have the emperor order the collection and destruction of all Jewish books. When Reuchlin, one of the leading humanists, spoke out in favor of the Talmud and other ancient Hebrew texts, he was tried for (and, eventually, convicted of) heresy. Hutten and a friend employed the weapon of satire in defense of Reuchlin and against the scholastic enemies of learning and scholarship. Their satirical *Letters of Obscure Men* provoked both approving chuckles and admiration from such fellow humanists as Thomas More.

Its serious aspects aside, the Reuchlin affair also was exhilarating for the young scholars. You catch some of Hutten's enthusiasm for his world of scholarly and scientific endeavors in what he wrote to a friend in 1518: "It is a pleasure to live. . . . Studies blossom and the minds move."

In 1521, at the time when the church reformer Martin Luther was called before the Diet of Worms to abjure his beliefs and teachings, Hutten, in support of Luther and the "cause of truth and freedom," published, in Latin, three so-called *Invectives*. In the third of the *Invectives* he admonished his own and Luther's enemies among the clergy with the words *videtis illam spirare libertatis auram*. Strauss rendered the Latin text into German by transforming the affirmative statement into a rhetorical question that Jordan translated into English as "See you not that the wind of freedom is blowing?" Stanford's motto is the abbreviated affirmative statement *Die Luft der Freiheit weht*.

For Hutten, what was the freedom whose wind was blowing? Clearly, freedom from as yet unreformed church orthodoxy, freedom from the Inquisition, freedom from Rome's worldly aspects. But freedom was also intellectual freedom, the freedom to engage in fearless inquiry and the freedom to speak your mind robustly and without inhibition. Hutten certainly used robust and even harsh language. The nineteenth-century Swiss poet Conrad Ferdinand Meyer composed an epic poem of almost two hundred pages, entitled "Hutten's Last Days," in which, as I discovered to my bemusement this summer, he rendered what Jordan chose for Stanford's motto as "The *harsh* wind of freedom blows."

The reasons for Jordan's interest in Hutten are easy to discern because as early as 1886 he had published an account of the life of Hutten that implicitly and explicitly tells us what David Starr Jordan considered important about Hutten and therefore about the "freedom" in "The wind of freedom blows." The opening paragraph of Jordan's sketch says much about what he himself valued. I quote:

> Four centuries ago began the great struggle for freedom of thought which has made our modern civilization possible. I wish here to give something of the story of a man who in his day was not the least in this conflict—a man who dared to think and act for himself when thought and act were costly.

Elsewhere Jordan writes that Hutten "was a man not of free thought only, but of free speech, and knew no concealment." Jordan also refers to Hutten as somebody who was "intolerant of intolerance."

Why, you started asking yourselves some time ago, is the new president telling us all this—or, rather, since this is informal California, you have probably been asking "Why is *Gerhard* telling us all this? Just because *he* was embarrassingly ignorant way back in March?" Well, that is part of it. My ignorance got me to read, and what I read impressed on me what a splendid choice Jordan and Stanford made when they invoked the "winds of freedom" as the short expression of principle to guide Stanford University. What does this principle entail? Permit me to make a few brief suggestions.

A university's freedom must be first of all the freedom that we take mostly for granted, though the humanists had to fight for it and others must still do battle for it even today: the pursuit of knowledge free from constraints as to sources and fields. Hutten and his friends rose up when they were told that Hebrew instruction and Hebrew texts should be banned because they were in conflict with the Christian message and mission.

Second, a university must be free to challenge established orthodoxy. Erasmus, Thomas More, and Hutten put forward their "new learning" in opposition to the ruling scholasticism that they found wanting. A university is the ally of change, and change is the ally of the university. The main task of the university is to question and to challenge fundamental assumptions and practices—that is, by implication, to favor change if these assumptions and practices prove to be wrong. The university's commitment is to knowledge and research, not to a particular content or program or to specific results. Only in one respect must the university be rigidly conservative: It must protect the openness, the rigor, the seriousness of its work in education and research.

Third, a university's freedom must be the freedom to challenge new orthodoxy. Just as traditions should not be embraced merely because they are traditions, the newest intellectual fashions should not rule just because they are new. While Hutten supported Martin Luther, he hardly wished the latter's teachings to become dogma. Erasmus, for his part, eventually broke with Hutten, whom he considered too radical. And Sir Thomas More has become *Saint* Thomas because he died a martyr defending the old faith against Henry VIII's new orthodoxy.

Fourth, a university's freedom must be the freedom of its members, faculty, and students to think and speak for themselves. A university must not have dominant ways of thinking. Hutten was, in Jordan's words, "intolerant of intolerance." No university can thrive unless each member is accepted as an autonomous individual and can speak and will be listened to without regard to labels and stereotypes.

Fifth, a university's freedom must be the freedom to speak plainly, without concealment and to the point—that is, without endless hedgings and escape clauses. As Jordan wrote, Hutten was a man not of free thought only, but of free speech, and knew no concealment.

Sixth, a university's freedom should include the freedom to take pleasure in the life of the mind. I quote again Hutten's enthusiastic statement from his own student days: "It is a pleasure to live. . . . Studies blossom and the minds move."

Addressing myself especially to the first-year students and speaking as a faculty member, I should like to emphasize that your education is primarily about "studies blossoming" and "minds moving." The enterprise is a joint one: You must take it seriously and we must take it seriously. Or, as Paul Freund, a famous teacher at Harvard, once said, education "is a two-way process—the rubbing of mind against mind for the benefit of not only the student, but of the teacher."

I am sometimes asked these days whether teaching will be one of my priorities as president. Of course, it will. As will be research. The question is well meant, but ill conceived. In the best universities—and you are at one of the best universities in the world—teaching, learning, and research are all *equally important* elements of the all-embracing search to know. This search to know takes place in the classroom, in the library, in the laboratory, in the study. It may even take place in the Main Quad. Your search to know and our search to know are interdependent: It is our task to inform and challenge you, and it is your task to question and challenge us and to seek out opportunities to do research with us so that the search to know may go on.

Seventh, the wind of freedom blows across national and cultural boundaries, it does not stop at them. Hutten, like many of his humanist friends, claimed the freedom to engage in fruitful contacts with whomsoever and wheresoever. His world was limited to Europe; ours comprises all continents. The anthropologist Marshall Sahlins has recently stressed that we are experiencing the formation of a world system of cultures, "a Culture of cultures," whose spaces are characterized by *both* differentiation and assimilation. I know few universities that are better positioned than Stanford to become a place of learning with a truly *inter*national and *inter*cultural character. We need to understand, appreciate, and value differences, while realizing that without a common thread holding us together, we shall be lost.

Eighth, the wind of freedom cannot blow in a closed and stuffy ivory tower. Members of a university community must not shy away from the social and political issues of their time, from shaping the social and political values of society, from engaging in public service. Public service is their freedom, indeed their *obligation*. It is not, however, necessarily the university's freedom. A university's freedom and obligation are to provide a forum for the most searching and candid discussion of public issues. But as one of the century's foremost First Amendment scholars, my much missed Chicago colleague the late Harry Kalven, has said, a university "cannot take collective action on the issues of the day without endangering the conditions for its existence and effectiveness. There is no mechanism by which it can reach a collective position without inhibiting that full freedom of dissent on which it thrives." This viewpoint arises "not out of a lack of courage nor out of indifference and insensitivity. It arises out of respect for free inquiry and the obligation to cherish a diversity of viewpoints."

Finally, teaching, learning, and research benefit not from stagnant air but from fresh winds blowing. There can be no fresh wind without highest-quality research. Mediocrity leads to nothing other than more mediocrity. In our pursuit of excellences at Stanford, let us not forget that Stanford, with the rest of the great American research and teaching universities, will become forgettable—and that means, will be doomed—unless the United States and we remain committed to the support of original investigation of the first rank, and the investments in education and training that go with it.

Apart from gathering the best minds and providing them with resources, hard work and a substantial measure of freedom in the setting of research priorities have always been among the conditions that make highest quality research possible. Good institutions and good work need a lot of breathing space. I worry that as we attend to the shortcomings of universities, we as a country are losing sight of the conditions that create good work and good institutions. We should also remember that burning the midnight oil, hard work in study and laboratory, remains the rule at Stanford and its sister universities even if those who see only shortcomings will not admit it. The research enterprise can easily be smothered by internal and external politics, pressures, and red tape. The wind of freedom has been a necessary, if not sufficient, condition for making our great universities the envy of the world. Without that freedom, that greatness is imperiled.

I return to you, my fellow first-year and my fellow transfer students, as we enter Stanford together. When David Starr Jordan decided to leave the Midwest to come to Stanford, he wrote to his mentor Andrew Dickson White, the president of Cornell, that he was prepared "to take whatever came." It is evidence of Jordan's fascination with Hutten that even at this occasion he quoted two lines from a poem by Hutten entitled "Hutten's Song":

> With open eyes I have dared it,
> and cherish no regret . . .

"I have dared it" was indeed Hutten's personal motto. May you and I, in the course of our Stanford education, frequently dare to seize the opportunities that Stanford has to offer us. If we do, we shall experience the pleasures that come from studies blossoming and minds moving.

Context

In 1990–91, Harvard University had conducted a search for the successor to Derek Bok. To my great surprise, it appeared that I was the runner-up to the Harvard Corporation's eventual choice for president, Neil Rudenstine. This had put me, as some would say, "into play" for major university presidencies. In Chicago, there were many who more or less assumed that I would eventually succeed

Hanna Gray as president of the University of Chicago. I, on the other hand, having been a dean and a provost, was not free from ambivalence about any university presidency, since I understood only too well the challenges and difficulties that university leadership positions pose.

On July 29, 1991, Donald Kennedy, president of Stanford since 1980, announced that he would step down as of August 31, 1992. At the time, Stanford was not part of my world. Stanford was, of course, much in the news, but I had then only one close friend at the university, the late Gerald Gunther, one of the country's most distinguished constitutional law scholars. According to a newspaper account, he nominated me in October 1991 for the Stanford presidency and called members of the search committee and Stanford trustees. Gerry supposedly said: "He is not going to impress you as the standard Stanford type. He's not a laid-back Californian; he comes with a German accent."

Stanford's trustees were bent on avoiding the speculations and leaks that had characterized the 1990–91 Harvard search, and Stanford conducted its search in complete confidentiality. I never applied nor did I hear from Stanford or talk to them until February 7, 1992, when four members of the search committee, led by its deputy chairman, James Sheehan, of the Stanford History Department, visited me at our apartment in Hyde Park to "discuss my views of Stanford and possible candidates for the Stanford presidency." There were no further contacts until March 5, when the chairman of the search committee, trustee John Lillie, and the board chairman, James Gaither, came to Chicago to ask me to meet with the entire search committee. This meeting took place three days later, on March 8, in Los Angeles. One week after that, the Stanford Board of Trustees voted to offer me the Stanford presidency, and I accepted on March 17, Saint Patrick's Day.

But for the confidentiality of the Stanford search, I would not have become the Stanford president. Had the matter leaked or had there been extensive speculation about it, I am convinced that pressures would have been brought to bear in Chicago that, in combination with Regina's and my own inclinations, would have made us stay in the Midwest. On the other hand, after the meeting with the Stanford search committee at a hidden office suite in Century City, Los Angeles, I considered the Stanford possibility in ways in which I had not done previously. Their quality, commitment, seriousness, and enthusiasm painted a picture of the challenges at the university that made me see Stanford as an extraordinary opportunity. After intense discussions, Regina and I did what, in light of our twenty-six years in Chicago and our affection for the University of Chicago, the city, and our many friends there, we had thought we would never do—return to the San Francisco Bay Area.

Stanford had celebrated its centennial in 1990–91. Organized in 1885, the university had opened its doors in 1891, during the same period as the founding of Johns Hopkins and the University of Chicago. All three universities had been deeply influenced by the scholarly emphasis that had spurred much of German higher education since Wilhelm von Humboldt, in 1810, had laid down his ideas for a university in Berlin. Symbolically, a statue of Humboldt's brother Alexander, the great naturalist, geographer, and explorer, adorns the outer wall of Jordan Hall at Stanford, along with a statue of Louis Agassiz, the Swiss-American Harvard biologist. Alexander von Humboldt had been Agassiz's mentor, and Agassiz, in turn, had furthered the scientific interests of David Starr Jordan, Stanford's first president. What Michael Polanyi once referred to as "the apostolic succession of scientists" thus finds an expression in that conjunction of the two statues with Jordan Hall.

Stanford's breakthrough into the ranks of the best universities in the United States and in the world, however, took place about half a century later. After World War II, the inspired leadership of Wallace Sterling and Fred Terman made Stanford seize the opportunities offered by the peer-reviewed, university-based, and federally funded research system that the federal government had put in place after the war. One of the more consequential government initiatives in American history, it had been Vannevar Bush's response ("Science, the Endless Frontier") to President Roosevelt's request that Bush develop proposals that could lead to "the improvement of the national health, the creation of new enterprises bringing new jobs, and the betterment of the national standard of living." Stanford excelled in garnering federal research support and improved its quality in all areas of the university, including those that the federal government was by and large not funding, such as the humanities and social sciences. By the mid-1980s, Stanford's undergraduate and graduate programs were much in demand, and applications and yield among applicants comparable only to the top Ivies.

On April 5, 1990, President Donald Kennedy gave a centennial address at the annual meeting of Stanford's Academic Council, essentially the entire faculty of the university. The speech, entitled "Stanford in Its Second Century," put forward a vision of "Stanford 2010." At the outset, Kennedy discussed the "somber background" against which the university's future had to be seen. That background included the 1989 Loma Prieta earthquake—the first earthquake to do major damage to the university since the San Francisco earthquake of 1906. (I continued to deal with the consequences for years to come.) In addition to Loma Prieta, Kennedy listed the waning of government support for science; "political resistance" to paying "the full cost" of research; faculty concern over the indirect cost rate and the size of the university administration (for the 1990–91 fiscal year, Stanford was proposing to charge 78 percent of direct costs as "indirect costs"—the highest overhead rate of any American university except for Harvard Medical School, which, in 1991, requested a rate above 100 percent); "storm signals" about rates of tuition increase; and "signs of mistrust and apprehension even from faithful constituents." Indeed, at the time Stanford prepared for its centennial year celebrations, Kennedy's administration had already started dealing with what he characterized as "the predominant challenge": the need to reduce size and expenditures through budget reductions and organizational change. The undertaking had been baptized "Repositioning and Simplification" and brought about expenditure cuts in the amount of $22 million.

On the academic side, Kennedy's speech placed the emphasis on a recommitment to undergraduate education: "The joint-product character of our enterprise has long been a source of strength to us: teaching and research are both important. But the relative weight has shifted over time, as the relatively new term 'research university' suggests. *It is time for us to reaffirm that education—that is, teaching in all its forms—is the primary task, and that our society will judge us in the long run on how well we do it.*" [Italics in the original.] Himself a greatly gifted teacher of undergraduates, Kennedy went into some detail about "what we must do."

There was one fleeting reference to what had become a major source of "mistrust and apprehension from faithful constituents." Kennedy said: We do not "argue enough, except in rare episodes like the CIV debate, about what ought to be the common intellectual property of educated men and women." The "CIV debate" (CIV stood for "Cultures, Ideas, and Values") referred to changes in Stanford's compulsory three-quarter humanities requirement for freshmen that had been undertaken by the faculty in 1988. Known as Western Culture since 1980, the requirement had come under attack from students and faculty who sought to draw more broadly from different strands of our own culture, and to increase understanding of cultural diversity and the process of cultural interaction. The fight was especially *against* "the" canon and *for* "the inclusion of women and people of color" in the course coverage. The Stanford battle, only one of many in the nationwide culture wars, had been especially intense and received much press attention, especially in connection with the participation of Jesse Jackson in a 1987 demonstration and the students' slogan "Hey, hey, ho, ho, Western Culture's got to go." Within one year of the beginnings of the inflamed debate that had been triggered by the publication of my Chicago colleague Allan Bloom's much bought (though little read) *The Closing of the American Mind,* the Stanford Faculty Senate voted overwhelmingly to rename the humanities requirement "Cultures, Ideas, and Values" (CIV) and to adjust the course goals in a multicultural direction.

Racial tensions among students on campus in the late 1980s had led to a new focus on minority issues and had caused one other major policy controversy of national significance to emerge at Stanford. In 1990, the Student Conduct Legislative Council adopted an "interpretation" of the Fundamental Standard that has governed student conduct since 1896. The Fundamental Standard reads: "Students are expected to show both within and without the University such respect for order, morality, personal honor, and the rights of others as is demanded of good citizens. Failure to observe this will be sufficient cause for removal from the University."

The interpretation was titled "Free Expression and Discriminatory Harassment." It spelled out when the face-to-face use of racial epithets or their equivalent would be viewed as "harassment by personal vilification" and, therefore, as a violation of the Fundamental Standard. All other forms of speech at Stanford were protected. However, what became known as the Grey Interpretation (for law professor Thomas Grey) raised the question whether university campuses should impose greater restrictions on free speech than were thought to prevail in the society at large. The first question I was asked at the press conference announcing my appointment as president pertained to the Grey Interpretation. I shall return to the issue in a subsequent chapter.

In discussing "ominous signs" in "Stanford in Its Second Century," President Kennedy mentioned "a growing conviction that constraints on the national resources that support original scholarship, particularly in the sciences, are becoming so binding that Stanford will need to invest more of its own resources in these activities." Kennedy did not know that, one month before his April 1990 address to the Academic Council, Paul Biddle, the resident representative of the Office of Naval Research on the Stanford campus, had written a lengthy letter to his superiors accusing Stanford of "abuse" and "distortion." For historical reasons, ONR is the government agency with cognizance over all expenditures of government research moneys at the university. Controversies concerning the cost of research and overhead charges subsequently engulfed Stanford and threatened the university in ways that made the Loma Prieta earthquake seem a minor mishap by comparison. Armies of auditors descended on Stanford, and ONR unilaterally reduced the university's reimbursement rate for indirect costs to 55 percent (thus causing a fresh $25 million shortfall in unrestricted revenues). The often inaccurate press coverage severely damaged the university's reputation, and, in 1991, Biddle filed a *qui tam* suit against Stanford that created a considerable financial exposure for the university, potentially in the hundreds of millions of dollars, for which he would personally share in any recoveries. Also in 1991, the university took severe beatings in the media and in hearings on indirect costs before a congressional subcommittee headed by Representative John Dingell.

On July 29, 1991, President Kennedy announced that he would step down. In his statement he said: "At present we are talking too much about our problems and too little about our opportunities. . . . It is very difficult, I have concluded, for a person identified with a problem to be the spokesman for its solution. We need to banish ambiguity and to look to the future as we resolve the problems of the past."

I spent much of the summer of 1992 researching, drafting, writing, and rewriting my inaugural address. That is, I did so when I was not meeting with individual trustees, senior administrators (especially president, provost, and deans), representatives of the faculty, and staff to prepare for my first year in office. As I assessed the situation in which I found Stanford (and myself), these seemed to be major problems: the indirect cost dispute and accompanying investigations and litigation; severe financial constraints and budget deficits in spite of the fact that Stanford had just successfully concluded its Centennial Campaign, the nation's first $1 billion university fund-raising effort; approximately $160 million of damage caused by Loma Prieta; tuition levels; the size of the Stanford administration; continuing controversies over affirmative action, sex discrimination, multiculturalism, and campus speech; science faculty who were unhappy about research funding and humanities faculty who were conflicted about the role and purpose of the humanities and arts in the contemporary university; and confusion, mistrust, and disenchantment on the part of a fair number of alumni. Finally, of overriding importance to me, as I had thought since my days as provost at Chicago, was the question of the relationship between "research universities" and undergraduate education. I found myself in full agreement with Don Kennedy's observations on this topic in his 1990 speech.

The *New York Times* began its report on my Stanford appointment with the words "Stung by more than a year of scandal . . ." The *Dallas Morning News* headlined a lengthy piece "Stanford a textbook case of colleges' ills, experts say." And, indeed, a fair number of the issues that Stanford faced it shared with the rest of higher education. Most of the media, however, did not see a "textbook" case so much as a series of events to which, once and for all, they had attached the label "scandal"—endlessly repeating details that were purportedly telling. When, in 1994, the government and Stanford resolved their disputes and the government acknowledged that it had no claims against the university for fraud or any wrongdoing or misrepresentation, the media coverage was, of course, minimal.

As to my appointment, both television and newspapers made much of the fact that I was the first outsider named Stanford president in twenty-five years, and some newspapers reminded their readers (and me) that Kenneth Pitzer's turbulent tenure (after he came from Rice University) in the late 1960s had lasted only twenty-one months. What was I to say at my inauguration? What was I *not* to say? What were my tasks?

Following the turmoil of the preceding years and the nervousness it had created about the university's focus, I considered it to be my primary responsibility to stress teaching, learning, and research. I tried to do this both explicitly and implicitly, through an emphasis on Stanford's history and by "extending" that history to the Renaissance—thus making Renaissance humanism, as it were, part of Stanford's history and relevant to the present.

This approach made it possible for me to offset the fact that I was an outsider to Stanford with the knowledge of the university's history that I had acquired in the months after my appointment. Nevertheless, in the opening paragraphs I embraced, as it were, the outsider status. Stressing it also made it possible for me to avoid programmatic details and a laundry list of promises that I might not be able to keep because of my only rudimentary understanding of the complex institution which I was to lead.

Since programmatic sound bites were not my style anyway, I decided to make the most of the fortuitous opportunity offered me by Jordan's choice of a motto. By bringing the humanities to life through my focus on *Die Luft der Freiheit weht* and on humanism, I attempted to take my audience of students (especially freshmen), faculty, staff, alumni, friends, and notables into a world that was far removed from what they probably had expected. I used the motto as a shorthand for bedrock principles of academic freedom.

This approach enabled me to deal with matters that had been long-standing concerns of mine, especially the robustness of in-and-out-of-classroom debate on university campuses. While "political correctness" had become and continues to be mostly a slogan of the political right, with little descriptive power, the phenomenon of self-censorship does exist. Most students want to be civil and fair and thus careful about not hurting the feelings of others. So do I. However, in a university, being too civil and too fair becomes problematic, if it leads to too much self-censorship in the presence of those who aggressively claim the moral high ground on whatever the subject. I had first noticed this self-censorship, including on my own part, when teaching law classes at Chicago. Matters of constitutional law pertaining to, let us say, discrimination or abortion, had become a minefield in American universities.

Stanford, in particular, had to deal with the implications of its rules on speech. Was there a de facto spillover from the Grey Interpretation into the classroom? Based on discussions with students to this day, I have little question that many students think twice before they let their speech become too uninhibited. My nine "suggestions" of what the wind of freedom entails were, in part, meant to address these matters. My impatience with the rigidities of both conservatives and liberals came through in my call for challenging both, *established* and *new* orthodoxy: "The university's commitment is to knowledge and research, not to a particular content or program or to specific results. Only in one respect must the university be rigidly conservative: It must protect the openness, the rigor, the seriousness of its work in education and research." The university's freedom "must be the freedom to speak plainly, without concealment and to the point."

There were other "suggestions" that were important to me and on which I elaborated in subsequent speeches. I shall return to those in later chapters. One issue, however, that I addressed in my commentary on the wind of freedom—an issue of great complexity and difficulty (probably too complex and too difficult for the occasion)—pertained to what had been one of the most wrenching question facing universities since the 1960s: What was the institutional freedom of the university to take positions on political issues?

I became a faculty member at Berkeley in 1964, a few weeks before the beginning of the Free Speech Movement. The student revolt at Berkeley, and subsequently at other campuses, involved two very distinct university issues throughout: first, the rights of students to use campus facilities for their antiwar protests ("when, where, and how"), and second, the question of the extent, if any, to which the university in its institutional role should be a political actor. This latter question was often intertwined with the first in that students frequently aimed their protest at university programs, officers, and buildings that they thought politically tainted. As universities were made vehicles for opposition to national policies, they were often severely damaged—their fragility rarely appreciated. After the Vietnam era, many called for universities to take sides on other issues—South African divestment among the most prominent.

In 1967, a University of Chicago faculty committee under the chairmanship of a brilliant First Amendment scholar, Harry Kalven, issued a *Report on the University's Role in Political and Social Action* in which it took the position that "the university is the home and sponsor of critics; it is not itself the critic," except from time to time when instances arise in which the society itself threatens the very mission of the university.

I quoted from the report in my inaugural address because I wanted to leave no doubt in anybody's mind that I did not think that universities were created to provide a platform for the political preferences of their presidents (or those of other community members). A few years later, a writer for the *New York Times* quoted from my inaugural speech and criticized my abstemious position for the timidity it supposedly displayed. He alleged that I had gotten the message that the trustees wanted me to be silent. I rather doubt that the Board of Trustees (that at any moment entertains a wide range of views about the public role of universities) had a clear view of the matter and preferred abstinence on my part. A set of notes (written by John Lillie, the search committee chair) about our meeting in Los Angeles (the only such meeting) does not refer to any discussion of this subject. My position was just that: *my* position.

To quote again from the Kalven Report: "To perform its mission in the society, a university must sustain an extraordinary environment of freedom of inquiry and maintain an independence from political fashions, passions, and pressures. . . . It is a community but only for the limited, albeit great purpose of teaching and research. It is not a club, it is not a trade association, it is not a lobby."

For me, the wind of freedom blew for purposes of teaching, learning, and research. I wanted to emphasize that it blew for all members of the community, including the undergraduates, including the freshmen. The university should be hierarchical only to the extent necessary. Academic freedom must comprise the freedom of students to challenge their faculty on academic grounds. Students must be encouraged to do so.

Stanford traditionally gathers freshmen and their parents at the beginning of their first quarter at what is known as "Freshman Convocation." In 1992, I asked that Freshman Convocation be canceled and that freshmen and transfer students instead be invited to the inauguration ceremony. My salutation, "Fellow members of the first-year class and fellow transfer students," was meant not to be cute but to go to the heart of the matter: The educational enterprise is a joint one. "Or, as Paul Freund, a famous teacher at Harvard once said, education 'is a two-way process—the rubbing of mind against mind for the benefit of not only the student, but of the teacher.' . . . Your search to know and our search to know are interdependent: It is our task to inform and challenge you, and it is your task to question and challenge us and to seek out opportunities to do research with us so that the search to know may go on."

Thus I foreshadowed what would be my foremost goal in the years to come, a goal that truly linked the university and its students, especially its undergraduates, to the pleasures that come when "studies blossom and the minds move." Our efforts to reform undergraduate education at Stanford began with my appointment of a Commission on Undergraduate Education, chaired by James Sheehan, in the spring of 1993.

Subtext

Four issues to which I would return repeatedly in the coming year and years were not mentioned in the inaugural speech: multiculturalism, diversity (though "diversity of viewpoints" made one appearance), affirmative action, and indirect costs. Everything concerning the indirect cost controversy between Stanford University and the federal government was in limbo, and there was no way I could say anything meaningful and convincing in a few sentences. Equally, there was no way I could deal with the other three subjects in a manner that would do justice to them before the several thousand assembled in Frost Amphitheater. Multiculturalism I did refer to obliquely and purposefully by speaking about Stanford's future as a place of learning with "a truly *inter*national and *inter*cultural character." A year later, I devoted an entire speech to the subject of "culture and cultures" and, in 1995, I extensively addressed the topic of affirmative action.

Among the letters the Stanford presidential search committee received in January of 1992 was one from Frank Tremaine, of Savannah, Georgia. He was a member of the class of 1936. I had not seen the letter when I wrote my inaugural address, but it expressed many of my feelings on the subject:

> On the basis of what I have read in recent years, mostly in Stanford publications, it seems to me that living arrangements, campus organizations and parts of the curriculum emphasize our ethnic and cultural (and sexual) differences, the areas of contention among us. Instead, I believe that residences, organizations and studies should promote understanding of our diverse backgrounds, our common problems and our common interests. We should be looking for ways to meld the best of our ethnic and cultural backgrounds, ways to compromise when they collide and to reconcile differences where they exist. We need unity for our individual welfare, for the good of the university we chose and the nation where we were born or which we or our parents adopted.

This is very much what I meant when I said in the inaugural address that the wind of freedom blows across national and cultural boundaries; it does not stop at them. "Hutten, like many of his humanist friends, claimed the freedom to engage in fruitful contacts with whomsoever and wheresoever. . . . We need to understand, appreciate, and value differences, while realizing that without a common thread holding us together, we shall be lost."

Postscript I

Die Luft der Freiheit weht was and is an appropriate shorthand for bedrock principles. Though alas, at the beginning of my inaugural address, I got my first encounter with it wrong when I asserted that James Sheehan provided it. A former trustee and close friend, Peter Bing, has corrected me since. He says that while he was driving to the small reception that took place on the day of my arrival, March 17, he was wondering what he should say to me. It occurred to him that Stanford had a motto in German. In the presence of Jim Sheehan, professor of German history, he asked me whether I knew that Stanford's motto was *Die Luft der Freiheit weht*. I then apparently turned to Jim Sheehan for confirmation. Thus, according to Peter Bing, it was he, not Jim Sheehan, who took the consequential step of alerting me to the motto that I have made so much of. Relying exclusively on one's recollections about the events of an intense and emotion-filled day, I should have remembered, is dangerous.

The use of the motto throughout Stanford history has been varied and intermittent. In May 1918, the university felt obliged to deny reports "apparently circulated" by "subtle German propagandists" that, "on the official seal of Stanford appears a phrase in the German language." The *Daily Palo Alto* wrote: "Unofficially, a motto in German has sometimes been used at Stanford, but Acting President C. D. Marx said . . . that it never was adopted by the trustees, that it appears nowhere on official University stationery or documents, and whatever use may have been made of it at any time has not received the sanction of the Board of Trustees or of the Academic Council of the faculty." I guess in order to make the point how unfamiliar they were with the motto, the editors of the *Daily Palo Alto* went on to misquote the motto as "Die Luff der Freiheit Weht."

At the same time, the *Stanford Illustrated Review* published an article by Jordan entitled "The Wind of Freedom." The article is prefaced by the following editorial comment: "German propaganda made it necessary for the University to issue recently a statement explaining that the University has no German motto on its seal. This history of the phrase by Chancellor Emeritus Jordan is timely as well as interesting." And interesting, if somewhat disingenuous, it is. I should like to quote the first three paragraphs.

> Some one in a spirit of illiterate intolerance has lately ventured to criticise Stanford University for its alleged German motto *"Die Luft der Freiheit weht"* (the wind of Freedom is blowing).
>
> As a matter of fact this is not the motto of the University, as it has never been officially adopted and does not appear on the University official seal. It is not the policy of the trustees to use a living language for this purpose, and the only motto I know to have been actually considered is *"Semper virens"* (ever green, or practically, ever growing), the scientific name of the redwood tree (*Sequoia sempervirens*), which is the central figure of the University seal.
>
> But the German phrase has a noble history in which Stanford is in a degree concerned.

Then follows an account of Hutten and the previously cited mention of Jordan's exchange with Senator Stanford about Hutten and the winds of freedom back in 1891–92. The article concludes with the sentence: "Meanwhile it is still true that 'the wind of freedom is blowing,' and it will in due time sweep over the whole earth."

It appears that the "alleged" motto that, at best, had been adopted by custom, though never "officially," returned to ordinary use no later than 1923. Just before the beginning of World War II, when the Stanford Alumni Association commemorated the fiftieth anniversary of the laying of the cornerstone for the university with a 250-page "pictorial record," the seal with the motto in German decorated the cover.

Over the decades, the disparity of symbols representing the university grew. The university, individual schools, and departments used several different seals on official documents, stationery, business cards, and licensed merchandise. Some included the motto, others did not. Even within departments use of the various seals was not always consistent. The overall situation could only be described as anarchic when, in 2002, a team of university staff members under Randall Livingston, the vice president for business affairs and chief financial officer, conducted a detailed review and analysis of the use and appearance of Stanford's seal in order to develop a coherent institutional identity and a standardized version.

The result was posted on the Stanford website and did not include the motto. I had been unaware of the administrative efforts until somebody asked me why the motto had "disappeared." Since the motto had never been adopted officially, the characterization "disappeared" referred only to my attempts to establish a tradition and employ the motto persistently as a shorthand for bedrock principles. Eight years of efforts seemed to have been in vain, and I made inquiries.

Randall Livingston wrote: "The motto is almost always dropped on the web because of low resolution and often dropped on stationery. Some reasons why people don't use the version with the motto? Some people think it looks cluttered, some people don't like the motto because they don't think it is 'official,' some don't like it because they can't pronounce it and some don't know what it means. . . . The design people uniformly find it hard to reproduce . . . especially on the web and when reduced in size."

A couple of meetings and exchanges resulted in, from my point of view, a happy end. On December 10, 2002, the Board of Trustees voted a "Resolution for the Adoption of an Official Seal of

Stanford University seal (Courtesy of Stanford
University, Stanford, California)

the University." The Sequoia stands in a simplified landscape. The
motto surrounds it and, at the bottom of the seal, the year 1891
appears.

Thus, at least for the time being, the motto is now "official."

Postscript II

As concerns the "nine freedoms" that I spelled out in the address,
for me, they served as starting points not for syllogistic reasoning
but for reflection about the implication of the various freedoms for
the life of the university, for faculty and students, that is, and for the
institution as such. At least one of those "freedoms," "the freedom
to take pleasure in the life of the mind," was more a call on the students present to seize the extraordinary opportunity they had been
given to participate in what Wilhelm von Humboldt called the
modern university's "unceasing process of inquiry."

I had first sounded a similar theme when I served as provost of the University of Chicago. Chicago has a tradition of inviting a faculty member to speak about the aims of education at freshman convocation in Rockefeller Memorial Chapel. I gave the Aims of Education Address in 1990, calling it "A Golden Age of Education." It expressed much of what I emphasized subsequently in my years as the Stanford president. In a way, similar to bringing the humanities and the Renaissance into my inaugural address as president, I provided a humanities perspective on the notion of a "golden age" and stressed the opportunities and tasks the students had ahead of them. Most of the text follows.

The notion of a golden age that once existed in a distant past is common to many civilizations. It may, for instance, be found among the Hindus. One celebrated version of it was put forward by the Greek poet Hesiod, who linked it to the reign of the Titan Cronus, the father of Zeus. In the Golden Age, according to Hesiod, mortals lived "as if they were gods, their hearts, free from all sorrow, . . . and without hard work or pain, no miserable old age came their way. . . . They took their pleasure in festivals and lived without troubles." Just like the Land of Cockaigne, it seems to have been a bit boring, though, alas, not for a very long time. Inherent in the notion of a golden age is that of subsequent decline. Hesiod described the descent from a Golden Age to a Silver Age, to a Bronze Age (an age of formidable men who killed one another off), to an intermittent age of Homeric heroes, and, eventually, to the poet's own period, which he called the Age of Iron and of which he had, to put it mildly, not a very high opinion. I quote: "Never by daytime will there be an end to hard work and pain, nor in the night to weariness when the gods will send anxieties to trouble us."

As Hesiod lived around 700 B.C. and did not embrace a cyclical philosophy of history, you can imagine where that leaves you and me—even worse off. He believed a time would come when "children, as they are born, grow gray on the temples, when the father no longer agrees with the children, nor children with their father, when guest is no longer at one with host, nor companion to companion, when your brother is no longer your friend as he was in the old days." You will recognize some features of our own times.

Hesiod's unrelieved pessimism did not prevent subsequent generations from discovering other golden ages: the Periclean age is considered the golden age of Athenian democracy; there is a golden age of Latin literature; the Siglo de Oro in Spanish literature gave us *Don Quixote*. In short, a golden age can be, as it were, subject-matter specific; it need not have paradisaic qualities all around.

Which leads me to the question of what the golden age of education, or more precisely "higher education," might have been. The answer depends on what about education we want to emphasize. If we were to focus on great teachers, one might argue that the golden age of education came as soon as 200 to 300 years after Hesiod's dismal Age of Iron, when in the short period of about 150 years, Buddha, Confucius, and Socrates began what in universities we call their "teaching careers." As distinguished from almost everybody else's teaching career, though, theirs have not yet ended, and it is likely that you yourselves will become their students—especially at the University of Chicago.

Of course, universities have golden ages as well. At all universities these tend to be located in the past, though usually not in the distant past. There are two reasons for this: one, the living alumni, and the other, the older faculty. Whether you talk to Chicago alumni or those of Harvard, Yale, Michigan, Stanford—you name it—they will almost invariably assure you that their alma mater never had a better, more challenging, more exciting faculty than when *they* were students. This phenomenon is, of course, dialectically linked to the fact that the very alumni you ask tended to constitute the best class the institution ever had—just as the University of Chicago class of ninety-four will be the best class we have seen.

The second reason that a university's golden age lies in the past is that the most prestigious, older faculty have had their own golden age twenty to thirty years earlier. Looking dispassionately at their successors, they find them competent, but lacking in genius, originality, and spirit. The tendency is human and all nigh universal, captured with irony by the father of one of my law school colleagues, who once said to his son: "The sad thing is that in a little while these will be 'the good old days.'"

Occasionally, a consensus emerges about what period or periods in a university's history deserve the designation "golden age." As far as the University of Chicago is concerned, there are three such periods. The first is the founding of the university, whose centenary we shall be celebrating next year. The second is the so-called Hutchins era—named for Robert Maynard Hutchins, who became president of the university at the incredibly young age of thirty, not much older than you are now. And a third golden age will be the years that began yesterday and that lead to your graduation. I shall take these various ages up one by one.

In the late nineteenth century, a prominent eastern educator wrote that placing a major institution of learning in Chicago was "the next thing to putting it in the Fiji Islands." Since he cannot have referred to the climate,

I assume he meant the level of civilization—a slur equally offensive to Chicagoans and Fiji Islanders. In any event, as is so frequently the case with eastern educators or, for that matter, midwestern educators, he was wrong.

It is often said that, like Rome, great universities are not built in one day. Chicago nevertheless miraculously accomplished that feat through the endeavors of William Rainey Harper, its first president, John D. Rockefeller, its founder, and the enlightened citizens who gave them their support.

Chicago was one of the first universities in the country to be founded expressly for the pursuit of both teaching *and* research. It has never thought the aims of education to be those of a finishing school, or, as President Hutchins once put it, "[We are neither a grade school nor a place] where nice boys and girls have a nice time under nice men and women in a nice environment."

I hasten to say that—whatever Hutchins's view may have been—I am not against being nice or, for that matter, against having a nice time. I strongly encourage you to pursue both. Nevertheless, your education is a serious enterprise for both you and us. In the best universities, education and research, teaching and research, are two sides to the same coin—the search to know. This search to know takes place in the classroom, as well as in the library and in the laboratory. This is why, at Chicago, we do not believe that there is a conflict for faculty or students between teaching and research. Your search to know and our search to know are interdependent: it is our task to inform and to challenge you and it is your task to question us, so that research may go on.

Alas, you, as well as I, know that the B.A. you will obtain at the end of your undergraduate years (and you *will* obtain it) will not uniquely qualify you for a specific niche in the complex division of labor that characterizes contemporary societies. I urge you to think of this fact not as bad news but as an opportunity to search to know without narrowing vocational or professional objectives. While it is not your last chance, you will never have another chance quite like it.

As I suggested, the small number of people out there who do not believe that, on the whole, the entire one hundred–year history of the university has constituted a golden age of education tend to consider the so-called Hutchins era the second golden age. Hutchins's leadership of the university began in 1929 and ended in 1951. There is a dispute among historians whether the full time span of his tenure as president should be given the attribute "golden." After careful study, I have come to the conclusion that in terms of Hesiod's taxonomy, the Hutchins period was not a golden age at all but is more accurately classified as a "heroic era," most of which was taken up by the "Battle of Chicago"—spelling the world "battle" with a capital "B."

Hesiod said about the Homeric heroes that they were also called "half-gods" and that there was "terrible carnage" at Troy and elsewhere. There is little doubt that to many Robert Maynard Hutchins became a half-god and that there was carnage at Chicago. What was the Battle of Chicago about? It was largely about you— that is, about whether you should receive a *general* education free of disciplinary narrowness or whether the discipline of disciplines should invade undergraduate education in the form of "majors" and the like. Hutchins was utterly devoted to the "life of the mind" in the more general sense and opposed early specialization. George Steiner, the cosmopolitan intellectual, playing Hesiod to Hutchins's half-god, characterized the resulting atmosphere, last year in the *New Yorker,* as "hammering excitement." As you can read in the college catalogue, the college was charged "to do the work of the University in general higher education." The role of the college was to complement the specialization of graduate faculties by discovering ways to connect the entire universe of knowledge. You do not have to be an archaeologist to find remnants of this program in the Common Core general education requirements that Chicago, unlike other colleges, never abandoned.

Many of you will have heard of the list of "Great Books" established by the joined efforts of Hutchins and Mortimer Adler. Reading them, to Hutchins, was "an act of piety." In Steiner's words: "To read, to reread passionately, to read 'in dialogue' is to advance [the disinterested, joyously obsessive pursuit of truth that is the sole authentic purpose of humane learning]. A great university is one in which the necessary arts of reading are central. Hutchins' Chicago was exactly that."

It is probably fair to say that among your future faculty you will find few who believe in Hutchins's particular list, its ethnocentricity, or the "great conversation" that Hutchins organized among the great authors of the great books. In undergraduate seminars of the Hutchins era, students were encouraged to get an education by reading the great books themselves rather than heaps of secondary literature about them; to relate the authors' views of universe and human nature to one another. Not infrequently this ended up in treating the great authors as if they interacted back and forth through the ages. I heard an alumnus of Hutchins's college say the other day that sometimes it seemed like debating Nietzsche's influence on Plato's critique of Rousseau.

While even at the University of Chicago many of the particulars of the Hutchins curriculum are not canonical anymore, in the college and elsewhere at the university one Hutchins legacy is very much alive: our commitment to "the arts of reading": to reading, to reading carefully, to rereading, to reading in dialogue.

Now, to quote the French social visionary Saint-Simon, "the golden age which a blind tradition has hitherto placed in the past is before us." As far as *you* are concerned, there can be no question that the coming years will be the golden age of education. The idea of speaking about the golden age came to me last spring, when I happened to read a book by Janet Coleman entitled *The Compass*. It is the story of improvisational theater that started on this campus and in Hyde Park in the fifties and influenced the art of comedy in America. You can still encounter its successors on and off campus. The students, former students, and hangers-on that started the Compass, the name of their theater, not only had a lot of fun, but they also experienced a golden age of learning and acting. It followed Hutchins's heroic era. Ms. Coleman describes the features of the early fifties in these words: "the cold war, the Red menace, the nuclear threat, the Lonely Crowd, Newspeak, and the spiritual conditions that support psychiatrists—alienation, anxiety, malaise and sexual repression." In short, an age of iron that for the Compass became pure gold because they made it so.

The next few years will be a golden age because the character of an age is determined not by Zeus but by us humans. Your choice of Chicago will enable you from the first day to participate in the work of a great research university while, at the same time, as James Redfield has put it, "belonging to a smallish College with an organization and purpose of its own."

These institutional conditions will reinforce the most important means you have available to turn your college years into a golden age: learning from one another, challenging one another. I recently read the memoirs of a member of our economics faculty. He observed that in the leading universities, the students learn primarily from one another. "They learn to impose higher standards upon themselves, both in the selection of problems to work on and in the adequacy of the solutions they provide to these problems." The author of this theory of learning is George Stigler, who in 1982 received the Nobel Prize for his work on the economics of information, and therefore should know what he is talking about. My daughter, Hanna, who graduated college last year, confirms Mr. Stigler's view.

These days it is often said that among the preconditions of a successful education is the availability of role models. It is more suggested than tightly argued that education presupposes an opportunity to identify with somebody who shares some distinct characteristic with us: gender, sexual orientation, race, ethnicity, national background, regional background, language, religion—to name the most important.

It seems clear to me that if members of a group to which one belongs, such as a racial group, are unrepresented in some specific or in all areas of society, this may indeed have a dispiriting effect as one considers one's educational aspirations. To the extent to which the role model argument attempts to make this simple point, I agree.

A role model, strictly speaking, provides an example, perhaps a compelling example, for how to play a role. If one closely examines the metaphor, a theatrical metaphor, its most important element turns out to be not the model, but the role, the character to be played. John Barrymore may have electrified audiences as Hamlet, and yet his was only one of many possible conceptions of the role. Henry Irving's, Maurice Evans's, and Sir Laurence Olivier's are other portrayals that come to mind. Any actor has indeed a range of choices available. Yet whatever the challenges and uncertainties may be that an actor faces in making out the contours and essence of a particular role, the actor may at any given time concentrate on the one assigned dramatis persona. By comparison, we all face the difficulty of having to play many roles simultaneously at all times.

Recall the beginning of my talk, when I quoted Hesiod's prediction of an age which would follow his own Age of Iron, "When the father no longer agrees with the children, nor children with their father, when guest is no longer at one with host, nor companion to companion, when your brother is no longer your friend as he was in the old days." Hesiod, like Homer and other pre-Socratics, spoke in terms of social roles: father, child, host, companion, brother. What he saw coming, in modern jargon, we would probably refer to as the "disintegration" of those roles: father and children no longer agreeing, guest no longer being "at one" with host suggests conflict about what these various roles demand. In our own age we do not any longer believe that the Great Director spelled out with precision the essence of even the male and female roles. We have a difficult time indeed as we attempt to distinguish those traditional contents of a role that are worth retaining from those that should be discarded.

Each of us has so many different roles with changing demands to play that most of the time it seems beside the point to search for a model for one specific role that itself can be played in various ways—just like Hamlet. To become a person—the word derives from the Latin word for "mask," that is, the character played by an actor—involves, after all, the challenge to become oneself in the roles one must play. This, incidentally, also applies to the role of college student in which you have begun to perform today. As I have suggested, it too is a role whose contours are not too clear—sometimes the student even turns into the teacher. There is, however, one aspect of the role of a student that cannot be dispensed with without abandoning the very role. It has to do with the fact that no university can thrive unless each member is accepted as an autonomous individual, without regard to his or her sex, race, or any other factor irrelevant to participation in the life of the university. Randall Kennedy, a law professor at Harvard, referred to it in a recent article as a scholar's "skeptical attitude towards all labels and categories that obscure appreciation of the unique feature of specific persons and their work." It would mean stepping out of the role of a student if one student dismissed another student's views simply because of that student's background.

Among those who understand education or, for that matter, anything else much better than I do, is Edward Levi, the former president [of the University of Chicago]. In conclusion, I should like to quote him once more:

> The excitement and brightness [of college] arise, I think, because of the willingness of the [unroutinized] mind, . . . if sufficiently challenged, to test the boundaries that convention has laid down. The result can be a partnership between faculty and student in which the faculty member is also challenged to try to

point a path through a subject matter, or to exemplify that subject matter in the more careful view of a particular situation. This kind of movement through a discipline becomes a demonstration in intellectual honesty—a demonstration that only makes its point when there is the sudden realization that intellectual purity is not naturally within any of us.

Your opportunities are golden. If only you make use of them, this will be a golden age of education—and, because of you, it will be for us as well as for you.

3.

Invectives

On Rendering Judgment at the University

———————————

Founders' Day, Memorial Church

MARCH 7, 1993

Text

Unfortunately, it was too late when I discovered yesterday that Jane Stanford would not have approved of my being in the pulpit on Founders' Day (and I remind you that the word "founders" in "Founders' Day" is plural in form). On December 28, 1904, Mrs. Stanford wrote a letter to President Jordan in which she told him that she had no objections to memorial services in March: "It seems to me that it would be very appropriate indeed to have the services held in the Church built to . . . my husband's memory, but under no conditions whatever would I wish it to be simply a secular service. An ordained minister should be invited to speak, as he ordinarily would from the pulpit." In accepting Dean Gregg's invitation to speak today I unwittingly committed a sin against one of our founders. I hope that the fact that ours is *not* "simply a secular service" will have redemptive value. And while I am not "an ordained minister," I eagerly should like to point out that the doctorate con-

54

ferred upon me by the University of Freiburg in 1964 is at least a doctorate in *both* the civil *and the canon* law. Furthermore, I spend much, if not most, of my time preaching. I would rely on the good dean's power of absolution. However, since he seems a cosinner, I am not sure that would be effective in this case.

My talk is entitled "Invectives." The most perceptive among the congregation have already guessed that I should like to return to the subject matter of my inaugural address—Hutten and Stanford's motto "The wind of freedom blows." In 1521, at the time when the church reformer Martin Luther was called before the Diet of Worms to abjure his beliefs and teachings, Hutten, in support of Luther and the "cause of truth and freedom," published, in Latin, three so-called *Invectiva*. In the third of the *Invectives* he, Hutten, admonished his own and Luther's enemies among the clergy with the words "Don't you see that the wind of freedom blows."

By returning to Hutten, I do *not* mean to suggest that Stanford University was *really* founded in 1521. If we looked at the matter not in parochial historical terms, *that* suggestion might not be so far off. However, revisionist history writing has its limits. No, there can be no question that Stanford University was founded by Jane and Leland Stanford as a memorial to their son Leland Jr.: surely one of the most magnificent memorials in history.

In the summer of 1992, when I worked on my inaugural address, I read a number of books about Hutten that made me aware of how woefully inadequate the twenty-five minutes available to me on October 2 were and how one-dimensional a picture of Hutten I was forced to present, given the many things I wanted and needed to accomplish that day. While my account was as accurate as I could make it, given that I am a nonexpert, it, by necessity, was an idealized one. Today, I should partially like to complete the picture. I say "partially" because once again the time is too limited and I shall restrict myself to a couple of items.

First item: invectives. When Jordan and Stanford chose "The wind of freedom blows" as the short expression of principle to guide

Stanford University, the context from which it derived was not particularly relevant. It had been taken from a polemic against the "cardinals, bishops, abbotts," and the like assembled at the Diet of Worms. The polemic was indeed full of rather robust invectives. There was nothing tame about it. Permit me to quote Hutten more fully: "Begone from the pure streams, ye unclean swine! Depart from the sanctuary, ye infamous traffickers! Touch not the altars with your desecrated hands. What business have you with the alms which our fathers gave to the poor and the Church? How dare you spend the money intended for pious uses in luxury, dissipation, and pomp while honest men are suffering hunger? The cup is full." You get the idea.

The words are as strong as the invectives issued by the Prophet Micah and by Paul in his letter to the Galatians [Micah 3, Galatians 5:12: the readings for the day]. Indeed, Micah's accusations from the eighth century B.C. are essentially identical to those of Hutten in the sixteenth century A.D.: Micah, like Hutten, inveighs against those who "tear the skin from off my people," who "give judgment for a bribe," "teach for hire," and "divine for money." Micah, like Hutten, addresses the clergy. Paul's call on "those agitators" to go and castrate themselves is also strong stuff. The invectives are part and parcel of Micah, Paul, and Hutten. Referring to Hutten as a "humanist" suggests a pale scholar sitting in his study. In reality he was an unabashed man of strong emotions and also prejudices, including many of the prejudices of the very age he did so much to transform. He was, as Stanford's own professor of Renaissance history Lew Spitz has called him, a "militant critic."

Second item: prejudice. Erasmus of Rotterdam, the greatest figure among the humanists, had been Hutten's idol. In the last year of Hutten's life, as an exile, really a refugee from justice, he passed through Basel, the Swiss town where Erasmus lived. But Erasmus refused to see him. The "quietistic humanist" (Hajo Holborn) who was siding with the Catholic Church against the Lutherans had no use for the once admired, but now too militant, Hutten. Hutten, deadly sick, published an *Expostulation* full of invectives against what he considered Erasmus's switch: "The Germans are not like this, but rather the fickle and inconsistent foreigners, who turn like a weathercock. One finds this sort in Italy, among your confidants, the Roman cardinals, where each follows his own inclinations and pleasures." Hutten then engages in a direct ethnic slur: "Or take those French Germans [a designation referring to Erasmus's Dutch compatriots] who abound in all your characteristic faults. Unless you moderate these faults, to us intolerable, all Germans will have to ask you to go elsewhere." Hutten was a German nationalist, much beholden to his own class, the lesser German nobility. He was prejudiced and did not shy away from what we would call stereotyping.

As I pointed out at my inauguration, Hutten's earliest claim to fame was his role in a celebrated controversy concerning the preservation of Hebrew literature against efforts to have the emperor order the collection and destruction of all Jewish books. Unfortunately, Hutten's courageous defense of humanistic values does not signify that he was free of anti-Semitism. The waters are made muddier by the fact that it was a converted Cologne Jew by the name of Pfefferkorn who led the cause against Hebrew writings. When another convert, also by the name of Pfefferkorn, was executed for a variety of alleged crimes, Hutten published a pamphlet repeating the allegations of "desecration of the host, murder of Christian children, maligning a saint, defacing an icon, and worse. He congratulated the Elector for having eliminated such a monster from the world" (Lew Spitz). The accusations he makes are of the stereotypical kind that later was used to justify pogroms.

Third item: Hutten died at the early age of thirty-five, devastated by syphilis. He had contracted the disease at age twenty in Leipzig. We do not know how. It may have been sexually transmitted (prostitution was widespread at the time), but under the prevailing hygienic conditions he may also have come by it by other means. A libertine Hutten was not. In the fifteen remaining years of his life he suffered greatly and accomplished everything, including the poetry that earned him the laurels of a poet laureate of the Holy Roman Empire, in spite of his sufferings. He even wrote a book publicizing a cure for what was known in Hutten's days as "the French disease." In the first chapter of this book he laments the name and fights stereotyping, as the French are, I quote, "a highly civilized nation," the "most amiable and hospitable people of our age." The opening pages also address the theory that the epidemic that started in the last decade of the century was God's punishment for the moral depravity of the period. Hutten displays his impatience with theologians who pretend to know God's will and firmly comes down on the side of natural causes.

After a few years of remission, the disease returned. His last refuge from persecution was procured for Hutten by the great Zurich reformer Zwingli, who saw to it that the Benedictine monastery of Einsiedeln granted him asylum on an island it owned in Lake Zurich. There he died in August of 1523, provided for in the spirit of Christian charity by Catholic monks.

Rendering judgment is a favorite activity at universities. Many who render judgment are impatient. Hutten, who was a hero to our first president, David Starr Jordan, today would fare much less well. Hutten himself certainly was impatient. He tended to classify people into friends and enemies, angels and devils. We also tend to ask: "Is he one of ours?" "Does she belong to us?" If the answer is presumed to be "no," we are only too inclined to issue invectives, to call for excommunication. I urge us not to pose these questions, but to ask instead "What does he have to say?" "Where is she wrong, where might she be right?" "What is good about her, in addition to what is bad about her?" "*On balance,* how does this life sum up?" Sitting in judgment is necessary and unavoidable. But judgment, especially judgment at a university, that is not based on making every effort at understanding, including understanding the context, is no more than an exercise in arrogance.

These considerations are applicable to our founders. Some of the panegyric heaped upon Leland Stanford in the last years of his life is hard for us to take seriously. Oscar Lewis writes that Stanford was compared to "Caesar, Alexander the Great, Napoleon, and John Stuart Mill, to the disadvantage of all four." I spare you even more embarrassing hyperbole. On the negative side, a member of the Central Pacific legal staff said Stanford had "the ambition of an emperor and the spite of a peanut vendor." Arthur McEwen suggested that the arch above the entrance to the new university should bear the legend: "With Apologies to God." The "robber baron" image, the controversies surrounding the building and the operations of the Central Pacific, no doubt were behind this latter invective.

And then there are the parents who were so brokenhearted about their son's death at age fifteen that they were literally overpowered by it. Within weeks of Leland Jr.'s death, the father, then in Paris, is quoted as saying: "This bereavement has so entirely changed my thoughts and plans of life that I do not see the way before me. I have been successful in the accumulation of property, and all of my thoughts of the future were associated with my dear son. I was living for him and his future. This is what brought us abroad for his education. Now, I was thinking in the night, since Leland is gone what my wealth could do. I was thinking since I could do no more for my boy I might do something for other people's boys in Leland's name."

I do not think we are unduly partial when we conclude that what the Stanfords ended up doing for other people's sons and daughters strikes a balance that, as far as the university is concerned, does not call for an apology to God. The faith expressing itself through love is perhaps not, as Paul would have it in his letter to the Galatians, "the only thing that counts." But it counts.

Context

Founders' Day (then "Founder's Day") was first celebrated on March 9, 1894, nine months after the death of Leland Stanford. When I spoke from the pulpit of Memorial Church, the ceremonies began

with a wreath laying at the 1888 mausoleum that houses the sar-
cophagi of the three Stanfords and whose gates are opened for this
one occasion a year. From the mausoleum a procession moved to
Memorial Church, built by Jane Stanford to honor the memory of
her husband and dedicated in 1903.

When Robert Gregg, then the university's dean for religious
life and the chaplain of Memorial Church, invited me to be the
speaker in 1993, I readily accepted because I had wanted an opportunity to round out the picture of Ulrich von Hutten that I had
drawn in my inaugural address: what better occasion than a "church
sermon"! After I had told him about what I planned to talk about,
Dean Gregg chose passages from Micah and Saint Paul's letter to
the Galatians as the biblical texts for the day.

While nobody had taken me to task for too positive a portrait
of Hutten, my scholarly conscience was dissatisfied with the incom-
pleteness of it. Thus I welcomed the opportunity "to set the record
straight." In doing so I was much indebted to books by Yale's Hajo
Holborn and Stanford's Lew Spitz about Hutten.

I also wanted a chance to say more about campus discourse.
In my inaugural address I had referred to a university's freedom
(meaning the freedom of students and faculty) "to speak plainly,
without concealment and to the point—that is, without endless
hedgings and escape clauses." As I indicated in the previous chapter,
I was concerned about self-censorship. The Founders' Day talk was
meant to reemphasize another point that was of great importance to
me and that I repeated over and over again in the years to come.

The 1980s and the first half of the 1990s were characterized
by a certain tendency in American universities to "demographize"
those who participated in debate. A person's gender or ethnic background or age was sometimes invoked to disqualify or qualify a
speaker on politically controversial subjects. On October 2, 1992, I
had said that a university's freedom "must be the freedom of its
members, faculty, and students to think and speak for themselves,"
and that "no university can thrive unless each member is accepted as

an autonomous individual and can speak and will be listened to without regard to labels and stereotypes."

For somebody whose English is accented it was a natural—one might even say a self-serving—point to make. Since I had gone abroad for the first time at age sixteen, I had occasionally experienced stereotyping in ways that members of minority groups could easily recognize. I experienced it even at Stanford when, for instance, one morning, when I reached my office, I found a sign posted to its outer door proclaiming my administration to be "Casper's Third Reich." But the point that I had made in the inaugural address and then elaborated on and varied in "Invectives" also reflected my view of the academic ethic. There is no rigor or freedom in a university if its members are ready to jump to sweeping conclusions on the basis of unchangeable characteristics or group membership of those who participate in the academic debate.

For me the most important passage in my Founders' Day "sermon" was the one in which I referred to Hutten's tendency to classify people into friends and enemies. "We also tend to ask: 'Is he one of ours?' 'Does she belong to us?' If the answer is presumed to be 'no,' we are only too inclined to issue invectives, to call for excommunication. I urge us not to pose these questions, but to ask instead 'What does he have to say?' 'Where is she wrong, where might she be right?' 'What is good about her, in addition to what is bad about her?' '*On balance,* how does this life sum up?' Sitting in judgment is necessary and unavoidable. But judgment, especially judgment at a university, that is not based on making every effort at understanding, including understanding the context, is no more than an exercise in arrogance."

Of course, classifying people into friends and enemies is common in many human interactions. The German political theorist Carl Schmitt argued that it was the very definition of politics. It can certainly be found at universities where, nevertheless, it is especially inappropriate. The university environment should stand, as philosopher Thomas Hill has put it, for moral humility, for understanding the contingent nature of many, though by no means all, values. A year after the talk at Memorial Church, we chose alumnus Stephen Carter, a law professor at Yale, as commencement speaker. The choice was controversial because Carter had been labeled a "black conservative." Carter discussed moral humility by referring to "the depressing rhetoric of demonization" that characterizes present-day political and moral discourse. He also referred to the fact that moral certainty can be horribly oppressive. "After all," as Carter put it, "Pol Pot and the perpetrators of the Inquisition were morally certain, too."

My "doing things with words," of course, was and is to a large extent illusional. There was little continuity of audience from Frost Amphitheater in October to Memorial Church in March and, over the years, I was probably the only one who cared about the continuity of themes, as I seized the various pulpits offered me to make my points. I did insist on the publication in the *Stanford Report* of speeches on the more important subjects and occasions, but I am not aware that anybody on campus read them. Some of my speeches were transformed into columns that I wrote regularly for *Stanford*, the magazine of the Stanford Alumni Association. Judging by what alumni would volunteer to me, as I visited their cities, those columns did get a fair amount of attention.

Postscript

The mausoleum for young Leland (with reserved spaces for his parents) was built of granite and marble in 1888 by Italian craftsmen. It preceded the construction of the Main Quadrangle and is located northwest of it on a four-acre site that was landscaped by Fredrick Law Olmsted. According to Richard White, in *Railroaded* (2011), the mausoleum cost about $100,000 (which would convert to roughly $3 million in today's dollars).

Richard White, after referring to the tomb and to Memorial Church, continues to describe the triumphal arch that had been erected at the entrance to the Main Quadrangle and decorated with a frieze:

> Originally a sculpted frieze showing the procession of civilization in America wound around a massive arch. It began with a female figure of Civilization giving a torch to Columbus and ended with the mounted Stanfords . . . entering California with a locomotive at their back. They entered through the Sierras, which were held up by titans. This represented a trip of exploration for the railroad that Stanford actually never took. In between Columbus and the Stanfords came Pizarro, Cortés, Washington and figures representing agriculture, industry, and the arts. The arch radiated hubris too great even for California. The earthquake of 1906 brought it down, and it was never rebuilt.

Richard White, a Stanford faculty member, employs the measured words of a historian when he passes judgment on the Stanfords: "The university displayed the emotional vulnerability of the Stanfords, but it also revealed an egotism and arrogance that remains astonishing even in a state not known for its reticence."

4.

Corry v. Stanford University

The Issue of Free Expression

MARCH 9, 1995

Text

On May 2, 1994, nine Stanford students filed a lawsuit—*Corry v. Stanford University*—challenging the Fundamental Standard interpretation titled "Free Expression and Discriminatory Harassment." The Fundamental Standard has been the measure of conduct for Stanford students since 1896. It states: "Students at Stanford are expected to show both within and without the University such respect for order, morality, personal honor and the rights of others as is demanded of good citizens. Failure to do this will be sufficient cause for removal from the University."

The Student Conduct Legislative Council put the interpretation—popularly known as the Grey Interpretation—into effect in 1990, spelling out when the face-to-face use of racial epithets or their equivalent would be viewed as harassment by personal vilification, and, therefore, as a violation of the Fundamental Standard. The interpretation relied on the so-called "fighting words" exception to the First Amendment. All other forms of speech at Stanford were protected. Nobody has ever been disciplined under this interpretation.

On February 27, 1995, the Santa Clara County Superior Court issued its decision in *Corry*. The court held that the Grey explication of the Fundamental Standard was unconstitutionally overbroad; that it did not proscribe all fighting words and was thus an unconstitutional viewpoint-based rule; and that California's so-called Leonard Law was constitutional. The Leonard Law is part of the 1992 State Education Code and bars nonreligious private colleges and universities from disciplining students for speech unless government could prohibit the same speech.

I should like to begin my comments on the case by giving my view concerning what the decision is *not* about. Various newspapers have quoted one of the plaintiffs as saying that this was a victory for academic freedom and free speech. If it was, I do not believe that it was needed. At a university that is committed to speaking plainly, without concealment and to the point, a ban on insulting fighting words based on group characteristics is not likely to have a chilling effect on almost all relevant speech. Academic freedom and free speech were quite safe at Stanford University before the decision. I came to Stanford after adoption of the Grey Interpretation, and my experience has been that debate about scholarly issues, as well as public issues, has been and continues to be uninhibited, robust, and wide open here.

Second, the decision is not going to unleash torrents of hate speech at Stanford. This university is characterized to a remarkable extent by peaceful interaction. In spite of occasional incidents that are played up in the press—indeed, universities are no ivory towers—there are few institutions in American society that are, comparatively speaking, more successful than universities at encouraging their members to cross bridges. The Grey Interpretation was meant to express our community's strong commitment to civility or, in the old-fashioned words of the Fundamental Standard, respect for "personal honor and the rights of others as is demanded of good citizens." Civility at Stanford will continue, with or without the Grey Interpretation. And harassment, whether accompanied by speech or not, including harassment that is motivated by racial or other bigotry, continues to be in violation of the Fundamental Standard.

Third, it is ironic that, while opposing the university's rule on First Amendment grounds, the court endorsed the Leonard Law. I thought the First Amendment freedom of speech and freedom of association is about the pursuit of ideas. Stanford, a private university, had the idea that its academic goals would be better served if students never used gutter epithets against fellow students. The California legislature apparently did not like such ideas, for it prohibited private secular universities and colleges from establishing their own standards of civil discourse. Religious institutions alone can claim First Amendment protection in this regard. However, I seem to be about the only person who finds that governmental intrusion troublesome and uncalled for. Therefore, as Justice Holmes once said, "If I am alone, probably something is wrong with my works." The *San Francisco Examiner* called my position a "laughable convolution." I guess the *Examiner* must be right.

I was born in 1937 in a country where racism had become government policy. I grew up in that same country as government and private institutions attempted to rethink civil society in the wake of the horrors perpetrated by the Nazis. Therefore I confess to possessing less certainty about absolute positions than do the plaintiffs in *Corry*. To be sure, rules such as the Grey Interpretation ultimately may be futile in fighting bigotry. But should a private university not be permitted to struggle with the issue in its own, if imperfect, ways? When I ask this question nonrhetorically, I am told that racists and sexists also invoke freedom of association. Well, so they do, and I have no difficulty acknowledging a compelling state interest in eradicating discrimination. Extreme cases, however, make for bad law, especially as concerns the fragile private sphere.

I disagree with the court's statement that the Grey Interpretation has nothing to do with the four freedoms of a university, as put forward by Justice Frankfurter in his famous concurrence in *Sweezy v. New Hampshire:* that is, a university's freedom "to determine for itself on academic grounds who may teach, what may be taught, how it shall be taught, and who may be admitted to study." Until 1992, the State of California also respected a private university's right to set its own educational policies. Almost all other states do so to this date. Congress a few years ago resisted the temptation to do for the entire country what the state legislature has done for California.

Principles of free speech are among those we most cherish, as Americans and as members of a university dedicated to the open, rigorous, and serious search to know. Because these rights are so important and our country takes them so seriously, reasonable people entertain different views about doctrinal details, while strongly supporting the essence of free speech. Constitutional scholars—indeed, Supreme Court justices, even the four that attended Stanford—disagree about the line between what the Constitution protects and what it does not. For instance, the plaintiffs and the judge in this case rely heavily on a 1992 decision of the United States Supreme Court, *R.A.V. v. City of St. Paul.* I might point out that Justice Scalia's opinion in that case had the support of only four other justices. The four additional members of the Court agreed with the result but disassociated themselves from Justice Scalia's reasoning.

After consulting with others on the matter and after listening to arguments on both sides, I have nevertheless concluded that, barring unexpected language in the final judgment, Stanford should not appeal the decision of the Santa Clara County Superior Court. I was not here when Stanford adopted the "Free Expression and Discriminatory Harassment" interpretation of the Fundamental Standard. Its passage by the Student Conduct Legislative Council after eighteen months of discussion and debate left many on campus feeling ambivalent about it. I share that ambivalence. I am completely committed to Stanford's motto "Die Luft der Freiheit weht"—The wind of freedom blows. I do, indeed, believe that Stanford should voluntarily agree to be bound by the principles of free speech.

However, such voluntary agreement to principles is not the same as being ordered by the state legislature to follow every twist of case law.

In a perfect world of unlimited resources, we might test the court's ruling further. We do not live in that perfect world. With respect to this particular case, I have come to the conclusion that Stanford's limited resources of money, time, and attention are best kept applied to the central tasks of excellence and rigor in teaching, learning, and research.

The 1990 interpretation was written narrowly as a statement of the university's belief that individuals should be free of harassment, intimidation, or personal vilification. Those acts have no place at Stanford or in any rational, civilized society. Among our most cherished values at Stanford are a belief in the power of reason, and in the right of each person to be accepted as an autonomous individual, free to speak and be listened to without regard to labels and stereotypes.

As I have said, we have never had to use the 1990 interpretation. Harassment, threats, or intimidation continue to be unacceptable. Should they go beyond what is protected by law, we will invoke university disciplinary procedures. Otherwise, we shall continue to do what we always have done. We shall counter prejudice with reason. The work of reason is hard work, as is the work of building and maintaining a great private university. I invite all faculty, students, and staff to continue the work of reason.

Context

If one viewed the matter with a sense of irony, one might say that *Robert J. Corry et al. v. The Leland Stanford Junior University et al.* pitted the (theoretical) freedom of students to utter racist gutter epithets against the (theoretical) freedom of the university to disassociate itself from students uttering such epithets. In my estimate, no student or regular visitor to the Stanford campus, comparing the situation before and after *Corry,* would have been able to make out any differences in the campus speech environment.

Seen more broadly, the case was a battle over the vitality and role of a nineteenth-century standard for student discipline in the life of a contemporary private university that is struggling with the complexity of virtue in a large, multiracial, multiethnic society. As sociologist Edward Shils has reminded us, no virtue stands alone; every virtuous act costs something in terms of other virtuous acts; virtues are intertwined with evils. As it were, all actors in the dispute over "discriminatory harassment" at Stanford had some virtue on their side. The battle was fought on a highly symbolic plane.

The warriors included the student plaintiffs in the court case, led by Robert Corry, who argued that their speech had been "chilled" by the campus speech rules as amended in 1990. They were truly "ideological" plaintiffs leading the charge against speech "codes" and political correctness. Their moral high ground was to force their alma mater to allow speech (certain epithets and fighting words) that the university considered unacceptable and thus "restore free speech."

Though defeated in battle, the authors of the Grey Interpretation, led by law professor Thomas Grey, also occupied moral high ground, since they had fought valiantly against "discriminatory harassment" while, at the same time, attempting to make the Stanford world safer for speech by clarifying the vague and amorphous Fundamental Standard. In the battle between "free speech" and "freedom from harassment and racist intimidation," they thought that they had struck an acceptable balance.

On the other hand, those colleagues on the Stanford campus, especially constitutional law professor Gerald Gunther, who had argued against new rules and the Grey Interpretation on the very high ground that allowing speech that we detest is the true measure of our commitment to free speech, were vindicated by Judge Stone's decision and by my—very reluctant—decision not to appeal.

California State Senator Bill Leonard, a Republican legislator from Orange County, originated the only statute of its kind in the country (it became known as the Leonard Law), to force private colleges and universities (religious institutions, of course, excepted) to abide by the First Amendment to the Constitution as if they were government. The fact that the addressee of the First Amendment is the Congress (and, via Supreme Court decisions, all other governmental authorities in the United States)—but not private parties and institutions—received little attention in the California legislature. The 1992 measure outlawed disciplinary action against student speech that "when engaged in outside the campus . . . is protected from government restriction" and gave students the right to injunctive and declaratory relief. The measure "against encouraging students to conform to a politically correct view" had for its goal diversity of expression. Incidentally, it was also made applicable to public universities and public high schools in spite of the fact that they were already subject to the First Amendment.

Finally, Peter Stone, the Superior Court judge, who forced what he called a "well-financed, well-organized, major international institution with ease of access to numerous forms of media" to drop its "speech code," pursued legal virtue by *first* determining that the Stanford rules would indeed violate the First Amendment (if Stanford were government) and *then* answering the question whether Stanford's disciplinary standards were subject to state regulation. To find an answer to this latter question, he narrowed his inquiry into Stanford University's speech and associational rights to the issue whether having undesired students would affect the ability of the university to express the views on which the organization was founded.

Such narrowing of the analysis would clearly have astounded the Founders and the university's first president, David Starr Jordan. The Founding Grant (in accord with the so-called Endowment Act that the California legislature had passed in 1885 to enable Leland Stanford to proceed on his terms) gave the trustees the power to fix the conditions on which students would be admitted.

The first year, *Circular No. 3* included a section on "Government of the Students," which was probably written by Jordan and which read:

In the government of the University, the largest liberty consistent with good work or good order will be given to the students. The University is not a reform school; its bounty is intended for the earnest and industrious student, and the indolent and unworthy will not be retained in the institution.

This rather forceful statement was amended, in 1895–96, by retaining in the *Annual Register* the first sentence and then substituting new language (again, presumably in Jordan's words) that, to this date, constitutes what later became known as the Fundamental Standard:

Students are expected to show both within and without the University such respect for order, morality, personal honor, and the rights of others as is demanded of good citizens. Failure to do this will be sufficient cause for removal from the University.

In 1897, Jordan clarified his views in a letter to the chairman of the Committee on Student Affairs that was, at that time, the disciplinary body of the university. Jordan wrote:

The number of students seeking the advantages of the University is constantly greater than we care for. . . . It is a part of the duty of your committee to eliminate unworthy persons from the rolls of the University classes. You have the authority to request the withdrawal of any student whose presence for any reason seems undesirable. It is desired that you should exercise this authority not only on those found guilty of specific acts of immorality or of dishonesty, but on any whose personal influence is objectionable. Those who are dissipated, profligate, intemperate, tricky or *foul of tongue* [emphasis added] should be removed, though no specific act of wrongdoing may be proved or charged against them.

While some of it makes one cringe, the passage makes clear, Jordan much preferred giving an unfit student the "opportunity" to withdraw from the university to the imposition of penalties. He did not want the university to stand "with rod in hand and spy-glasses on its nose." That, to his mind, would do little in the way of moral training.

In both, the area of academics and the area of morals, Jordan's theory was a complex mix of liberalism and an ethic of responsibility. Freedom in personal development, by freely choosing one's area of study and freely establishing relationships with professors, on the one hand, was combined with accountability for the use one made of the university's resources and the responsibility one showed as a citizen of the institution, on the other.

The Care and Culture of Men was Jordan's title for an address to Stanford's "pioneer class," the class of 1895. The title was taken from John Emerson's observation that the best political economy is care and culture of men. The address highlighted the importance of education fitted to individual needs. It stressed education as strengthening individual character, "the growth of the power of choice." Said Jordan: "The best political economy is the care and culture of men. The best-spent money of the present is that which is used for the future. . . . The university stands for the future." This view of the university as "the best political economy" for the future implied that the money spent at present should indeed be spent carefully.

In a section of the 1899–1900 *Annual Register* that was now entitled "Conduct of Students," a paragraph was added to the 1896 formulation that elaborated the university's educational mission, very much in accord with Jordan's views of the matter:

> The primary purpose of the University, as set forth by its founders, is to train young men and young women "for personal success and direct usefulness in life." "Success"

and "usefulness," as here understood, involve character and effectiveness; and the resources of the university are directed toward the development of these qualities, so that every graduate may do some useful thing honestly and effectively. Each student, therefore, is expected and encouraged to work toward some definite end in the choice of his studies. Students unable or unwilling to do serious work, looking toward a definite end, are not welcomed and will not be retained in the University.

What all of this suggests is that, in the eyes of Stanford's founding generation, execution of the university's purposes and trust included the university's power, almost need, to disassociate itself from students who were not willing to live by the university's code. That a hundred years later the university would be forced by the state of California to accept as "good citizens" those who would use gutter epithets against their minority fellow university citizens suggests how anemic the concept of private ordering and the freedom of association has become. In California's way of viewing things, only religious institutions have the continuing right to impose rules about inappropriate speech.

This is, of course, not to say that the Grey Interpretation was desirable or workable. As my former Chicago law colleague Richard Epstein likes to say, the question who may lay down rules comes before the question what, if any, rules to lay down.

At the end of the nineteenth century, subtle concerns like this were not on the agenda when it came to student discipline. Of the traits Jordan referred to in his letter about discipline from 1897—"dissipated, profligate, intemperate, tricky or foul of tongue"—intemperance was the issue of the time and caused endless problems. In 1911, students (then the "Women's Conference" and the "Men's Conference," respectively) assumed responsibility for student conduct and for maintaining university standards. This responsibility was strengthened in 1921 when the Honor Code, as a special application of the Fundamental Standard, was first established. The institutional details and subsequent developments are of no interest here (in 1996–97, I was concerned with restoring to students their central role in establishing judicial policy and adjudicating cases).

In connection with the campus disturbances brought about by the Vietnam War, Stanford (the Faculty Senate), in 1967, adopted a Policy on Campus Disruption. The policy was meant to reconcile free speech with the objective "to maintain an atmosphere conducive to scholarly pursuits." Applicable to faculty, students, and staff, the policy prohibited disruption of university activities and obstruction to the movement of people.

Its major test came when President Richard Lyman moved to dismiss Professor Bruce Franklin from his tenured position in the English Department for having, in 1971, among other charges, incited protesters to interfere with the functioning of the university's computer facility. The faculty-elected Advisory Board concurred with President Lyman, but, before doing so, explicitly bound itself to follow the First Amendment. It said that Professor Franklin should have "no less protection of his constitutional rights at Stanford than that to which he could be entitled as a member of the faculty at a state university."

This rule had far-reaching implications. Subsequent debates about the scope of free speech on campus became debates about the exact interpretation of Supreme Court precedents, most of them originating from cases that had nothing to do with the institutional settings or educational missions of universities, especially private ones. In a Faculty Senate debate in 1989 concerning the then-proposed interpretation of the Fundamental Standard, Tom Grey, according to the Senate minutes, expressed ambivalence. He was not sure, he said, that Stanford should bind itself, in its disciplinary procedures, to every detail of current judicial interpretations of the First Amendment. "One of the privileges of a private university is not to be 'stuck' with whatever the courts happen to be doing in a particular decade." Alas, Stanford did get stuck with every detail and whatever the courts happened to be doing in a particular decade. Before the Leonard Law, it, in essence, did so voluntarily. Professor Grey relied on his reading of Supreme Court precedent.

I should now like to turn to the disputes that led to the Grey Interpretation of the Fundamental Standard from 1896.

There was one event that, more than anything else, contributed to the sense that Stanford needed to be more specific when it came to certain speech. At the beginning of the fall quarter in 1988, two white freshmen, one black sophomore, and several other students had a dorm debate about music and about racial purity. It took place at Ujamaa, the African-American theme house. At Stanford, theme residences are not confined to students of the theme group (they should provide no more than 50 percent of the residents), and white freshmen had been assigned to live there. The debate was apparently quite heated, and the black sophomore asserted that all music was black and that Beethoven had been a mulatto. The next day, the two white students, "stone drunk," removed a Stanford Symphony recruitment poster that had a large image of Beethoven on it, and altered it to make Beethoven look black. They then taped the poster next to the door that led to the black student's room. In the followings weeks, another poster was defaced by scrawling the word "Niggers" across it, while other messages suggested that nonblacks should leave Ujamaa, "our home," because they were not welcome. It was never determined who was responsible for these latter acts.

The reaction to the Beethoven poster led to emergency house meetings, to the identification of the perpetrators, and to a public event where the two white students appeared and apologized in a manner that was considered by many as "arrogant" and "insincere." The black student also spoke and said that the defaced Beethoven poster was more than just a derogatory racial poster but that it represented racism in general and reminded him of all the racial things that had happened back home in Chicago and at Stanford. The confrontation, attended by about one hundred students, ended in chaos.

On January 18, 1989, the university issued a detailed report on the incident (from which all of the facts above were taken), and on February 8, John Schwartz, the university's general counsel, and Iris Brest, associate general counsel, issued a statement that reviewed the history of campus speech controversies and rules and concluded that the two students who had defaced the Beethoven poster had violated neither the Policy on Campus Disruption nor the Fundamental Standard more generally:

> It appears from the Report that the two students involved in the Ujamaa episode did intend to produce a ludicrous, racial caricature of blacks. . . . But there was nothing on the caricature, nor does the Report suggest that the poster was intended, to threaten or defame any particular student or students. What remains, then, even if the two students knew how the caricature would be perceived, is racially offensive speech directed, perhaps, to members of a race generally.
>
> Under these circumstances . . . the standards mentioned at the outset counsel against seeking disciplinary action: there is no evidence of the intent necessary to prove a violation of the Policy on Campus Disruption or the Fundamental Standard; interpreting those rules consistent with First Amendment principles, there was no violation, even apart from motivation. And again, the conduct was expression, which the University seeks to permit to the greatest extent possible.

This position led directly to efforts by the Student Conduct Legislative Council (an official body composed of faculty members and students) to develop a prohibition of "discriminatory harassment." The Council, on March 1, 1989, proposed "Interpretations and Applications of the Fundamental Standard in the Area of Diversity" that focused on "personal abuse" and "group defamation."

The language employed was criticized sharply by law professors Cohen and Gunther and by former president Richard Lyman as not being in accord with First Amendment law. Lyman wrote: "Surely this willingness on the part of a student-faculty committee to rewrite constitutional principles at the drop of a hat is risky in the extreme and perhaps a bit arrogant."

New proposals were developed with the help of Tom Grey. They narrowed the scope of the prohibition to so-called fighting words, which were defined as words or other symbols commonly understood to convey, in a direct and visceral way, hatred or contempt for people subject to pervasive discrimination on the basis of their personal characteristics. Illustrations were calling another student "kike," "nigger," or "faggot."

After eighteen months of campus discussion, the Student Conduct Legislative Council adopted the Grey Interpretation, and President Kennedy decided not to veto it. He would have had the authority to do so under "extraordinary circumstances."

The "Fundamental Standard Interpretation: Free Expression and Discriminatory Harassment" was a lengthy statement that emphasized Stanford's commitment to the principles of free inquiry and free expression. It also emphasized the university's commitment to principles of equal opportunity and nondiscrimination, especially its commitment to prevent a "hostile environment" due to harassment of students on the basis of their sex, race, color, handicap, religion, sexual orientation, or national and ethnic origin. The "hostile environment" reference Professor Grey had carried over from the legal obligation that employers have under employment law to prevent discriminatory harassment. This restriction of discipline to cases of *discriminatory* harassment became part of the undoing of the Fundamental Standard Interpretation, since Judge Stone saw this as "content-based" regulation of speech—an especially suspect category of First Amendment law.

The crucial language in the "Interpretation" read:

Speech or other expression constitutes harassment by
personal vilification if it

    a) is intended to insult or stigmatize an individual or
      a small number of individuals on the basis of their
      sex, race, color, handicap, religion, sexual orienta-
      tion, or national and ethnic origin; and
    b) is addressed directly to the individual or individuals
      whom it insults or stigmatizes; and
    c) makes use of insulting or "fighting" words or non-
      verbal symbols.

Fighting words were defined as those "which by their very utterance inflict injury or tend to incite an immediate breach of the
peace." The words in quotes had been taken from a by then almost
fifty-year-old unanimous decision of the United States Supreme
Court in *Chaplinsky v. New Hampshire* that has been neither explicitly overruled nor explicitly reaffirmed by the court in spite of
otherwise momentous changes in its First Amendment jurisprudence. Judge Stone took the position that Supreme Court decisions
subsequent to *Chaplinsky* had narrowed its rule to speech that tended
to result in immediate violence. The Grey Interpretation therefore,
he concluded, suffered from being too broad.

While Judge Stone considered it both too narrow and too
broad, for all practical purposes the Grey Interpretation was quite
protective of speech. For instance, the "Beethoven is black" poster
would not have been found to violate the Fundamental Standard
Interpretation. When the student-published *Stanford Review,* in
1994, instituted a feature called "Smoke Signals" about "goings-
on" on campus and bearing a caricature of a Native American, I
came under pressure to move against the caricature. I pointed out
to the Student Senate (before the Superior Court decision had come
down) that the *Review*'s feature was protected by the Grey Interpretation of the Fundamental Standard.

Indeed, no disciplinary action was ever taken under the Grey Interpretation in the five years of its existence. Could it have had, as Corry and his fellow plaintiffs insisted, a "chilling effect"? Possibly. The problem with arguments based on "chilling effect" (and I have made them myself) is that most of the time they are difficult to prove.

Throughout my years as president, I was much more concerned about excessive self-censorship by students wanting to be "civil." As I had emphasized in my commentary on the Stanford motto in my inaugural address: "A university must not have dominant ways of thinking." I also stressed "the freedom to speak plainly, without concealment and to the point—that is, without endless hedgings and escape clauses."

On the other hand, by taking into consideration that certain forms of expression may by their very utterance inflict injury, the Fundamental Standard Interpretation emphatically said that, in a decent community, there is no room for "discriminatory harassment," no social value is attached to gutter epithets. There is no more emphatic way to make that point than to back it up with sanctions— at least in theory.

In practice, the Fundamental Standard Interpretation was an awkward instrument. How was the decision to charge a student going to be made? How was one going to decide that an expression amounted to a "fighting word"? Whose standards would govern this determination? How was one to prove what intent? Had I been at Stanford in 1989, I probably would have associated myself with Richard Lyman, who, in March of that year, warned against being panicked by an ugly situation that is simply not amenable to successful treatment through legislation and policing. Ironically, though, the alternative to what Lyman called a "quagmire of litigious acrimony"—educational efforts—have their own shortcomings if they impose new orthodoxies, dominant ways of thinking. Nowadays the university handles "acts of intolerance" through a reporting and educational mechanism that asks whether there is a "teachable moment."

My decision not to appeal was a difficult one. I remind the reader that Judge Stone of the Santa Clara County Superior Court held that the Grey explication of the Fundamental Standard proscribed only discriminatory fighting words and was thus an unconstitutional viewpoint–based rule, and that it was too broad in prohibiting fighting words that did not tend to result in immediate violence. He also held that the Leonard Law was constitutional.

As to the latter point, Stanford, a private university, for better or for worse had the idea that its educational goals would be served if students were not allowed to employ racial epithets to vilify fellow students. That, in and of itself, struck me as raising important questions of freedom for institutional speech and institutional freedom of association.

I was taken aback by the fact that most people did not seem to care about what troubled me then and continues to trouble me today. One would have expected that true conservatives would rally around the private university's freedom of association. Quite to the contrary, the conservative plaintiffs and their supporters invoked the power of the state to impose their ideological preferences on their alma mater. But at the same time, many true liberals unthinkingly concluded that what is the law for public institutions must be the law for Stanford.

A thoughtful alumnus, in a letter, articulated a widespread view of the matter:

> The principle of equal protection, barring, for example, race and gender discrimination, originally applied only to the government, like the First Amendment and other constitutional standards. "Private" institutions were free to practice racism. But our society made a historic decision, through various federal and state civil rights statutes, to extend that principle to private institutions that

receive public support, backed up by the enforcement mechanism of judicial review. I can see no principled basis for treating the right to free speech as somewhat less worthy of protection, at least in the context of the university, where it is an essential attribute of academic freedom. I think the Leonard Law is very much in the admirable tradition of civil rights statutes.

The letter illustrates a danger of syllogistic reasoning. The alumnus's argument had the following structure: Private institutions may be obligated to respect civil rights to the same extent as government; the right to freedom of speech is a civil right (like the right to equal protection); therefore, a university may be forced to respect the freedom of speech of a student to the same extent as government. The undifferentiated major premise is highly questionable. I would argue that there is a difference between not being permitted to discriminate on the basis of, for instance, race, on the one hand, and on the basis of speech, on the other. While it is possible to be categorical about race discrimination, government is not permitted to be categorical about a private university's educational mission. When the government determines how a university's educational mission should be understood and implemented, it goes to the very core of First Amendment rights of private actors. The freedom of ideas, of speech, of association belongs to the institution as much as it belongs to the individual. We seem to have arrived at a situation where we (still) recognize diverse views about religion as a basis for institutional autonomy, but not diverse secular views about what matters in education. That strikes me not only as dangerous but as diminishing the marketplace of ideas.

In spite of my strong reservations, I decided not to appeal. It did not seem appropriate to spend Stanford's then very limited resources of money, time, and attention to fight a case that, given the superficiality of the debate in the media and public, was portrayed as involving only the legitimacy of what hyperbolically were referred to as "speech codes." An appeal would not have been seen as touching deeper questions about educational autonomy of secular private institutions and about the constitutionality of the Leonard Law.

Postscript

My closest friend at Stanford, ten years my senior, was Gerald Gunther, the leading constitutional law scholar. He died, at age seventy-five, on July 30, 2002. His subtlety, situation sense, learning, and professionalism were unsurpassed by any other teacher of constitutional law. None was taken more seriously by Supreme Court justices and by his colleagues. Gerry strongly opposed the Grey Interpretation. I made reference to that fact in my remarks at the memorial service for Gerry. May they serve as a coda for this chapter.

In the spring of 1982, Oxford University Press published a book called *The Brandeis/Frankfurter Connection: The Secret Political Activities of Two Supreme Court Justices*. As the title suggests, Oxford saw the book as a muckraking sensation; so did the *New York Times*. Gerry, who had read the work in a respectable format, that is, as a Ph.D. dissertation, despaired at the publicity. Phil Kurland, another Brooklynite and then my Chicago colleague and friend, weighed in with a review in which he was critical of the publicity, but also expressed criticisms of the political activities of *Professor* Frankfurter.

Gerry and I corresponded about the matter and about Phil Kurland's review. It led Gerry to send me "one of his favorite Learned Hand passages." Permit me to quote from that passage because it captures what Gerry himself believed deeply and what he and I shared in our approach to constitutional law and to academic life. This is what Learned Hand had to say upon receiving an LL.D. from Harvard:

I am thinking of what the scholar imposes upon himself; better, perhaps, of what he may fail to impose upon himself; of those abnegations which are the condition of his preserving the serenity in which alone he can work; I am thinking of an aloofness from burning issues, which is hard for generous and passionate natures, but without which they almost inevitably become advocates, agitators, crusaders, and propagandists.

You may take Martin Luther or Erasmus for your model, but you cannot play both roles at once; you may not carry a sword beneath a scholar's gown. . . . Luther cannot be domesticated in a university.

Gerry was no Martin Luther. Rather, availing myself of the metaphorical contrast employed by Judge Hand, I like to think of Gerry as the "Erasmus" of American constitutional law. Erasmus was the greatest scholar of the northern Renaissance, and his primary commitment was to scholarship. Nevertheless, he remained not aloof, as Hand's comparison might suggest, when the institutions he cared about, especially, in his case, the church, were abused by those in power.

Gerry's primary commitment, likewise, was to scholarship, although he, too, did not stand aside when something went wrong with the institutions about which he cared, most prominently the Constitution, but also the university. His scholarly standards were exacting and his overall approach to the law subtle and humanistic, learned, reflective, and skeptical. His casebook, through which I learned to teach constitutional law and which was the foundation of a friendship that lasted almost four decades, places Supreme Court cases and constitutional problems in a context that is both historical and philosophical and that gives the reader Gerry's own sense that the law is a worthy subject matter, to be taken seriously, and one which is not altogether open to manipulation, by law teacher, student, lawyer, or judge.

Gerry Gunther here at Stanford, Paul Freund at Harvard, Alexander Bickel and Charles Black at Yale, Herbert Wechsler at Columbia, Philip Kurland at Chicago—to mention those of our former colleagues who clearly have become members of the "Supreme Court of History"—were wary of too frequent crossings of the line between "constitution as ideology" and "ideology as constitution." They understood that the American concept of the legitimacy of government is closely tied to the Constitution. They did not believe that "anything goes." To Gerry, the Constitution was not a tool but a guide. As Kenneth Karst has said, "He kept us all honest."

Apart from being a scholar and humanist in his approach to constitutional law, Gerry was one of the country's great constitutional lawyers in the technical sense of the word. His professionalism remained undiminished until the very end. Gerry and I were coeditors of a series of landmark cases of the United States Supreme Court. Six weeks before his death, he sent me a five-page handwritten memo about the 2002 term in preparation for a meeting we had the following day in his office. We were still talking about the term, at his home, the last time I saw him on July 19. . . .

Gerry cared deeply about Stanford and took his university citizenship as seriously as anybody, especially during the unrest of the late sixties and early seventies, when so many tried to leverage the university for their purposes. His "hero" from those days, as he repeated only recently, was our then president Dick Lyman. Twenty years later, he was equally concerned when Stanford adopted rules that restricted some student speech under the so-called Fundamental Standard governing student conduct.

I should like to quote from the views Gerry expressed to the Student Conduct Legislative Council:

> I am deeply troubled by current efforts—however well-intentioned—to place new limits on freedom of expression at this and other campuses. Such limits are not only incompatible with the mission and meaning of a university; they also send exactly the wrong message from academia to society as a whole. University campuses should exhibit greater, not less freedom of expression than prevails in society at large. . . .
>
> The proper answer to bad speech is usually more and better speech—not new laws, litigation, and repression. . . .
>
> I received my elementary education in a public school in a very small town in Nazi Germany. There I was subjected to vehement anti-Semitic remarks from my teacher, classmates and others. . . . I can assure you that they hurt. More generally, I lived in a country where ideological orthodoxy reigned and where the opportunity for dissent was severely limited.
>
> The lesson I have drawn from my childhood in Nazi Germany and my happier adult life in this country is the need to walk the sometimes difficult path of denouncing the bigot's hateful ideas with all my power, yet at the same time challenging any community's attempt to suppress hateful ideas by force of law.
>
> Obviously, given my own experience, I do *not* quarrel with the claim that words *can* do harm.

Gerry's steadfastness is all the more challenging given that the Nazis quickly went beyond speech and would have killed Gerry and his family had they remained in Usingen, the family's Hessian hometown for centuries. To the fact that Gerry's father, in 1938, finally agreed with his eleven-year-old son's urgent desire to leave Germany, the United States owes one of the greatest careers in American constitutional law in the twentieth century. And I, born in Germany ten years after Gerry, owe to it a friendship that changed my life.

All of us are thankful for what Gerry did for the Constitution, for legal education, for scholarship, for the university, for his colleagues and students throughout the country, for his friends. We so much wish it all had lasted longer than seventy-five years, but—as Gerry himself said to some of us during his last weeks—its ominous beginnings notwithstanding, his was a life of consequence and richly satisfying. We thank you, Gerry, for a legacy that is so much stronger than our tears.

5.

Concerning Culture and Cultures

Campus Diversity

Welcome to the Class of 1997 and Their Parents,

Frost Amphitheater

SEPTEMBER 23, 1993

Text

Members of the Stanford college class of 1997 and those among you who have had the splendid good sense to transfer to Stanford: On behalf of the university's faculty and staff, and your fellow students, both undergraduate and graduate, I warmly welcome you. We have looked forward to your presence with pleasurable anticipation because we know, on the basis of what we have learned about you, that you will be superbly qualified to test our abilities.

Equally warmly I welcome parents, other relatives, and friends who have come along to lessen the apprehensions that our freshmen might have. For many parents this is not the easiest of tasks since they themselves are full of apprehension about this rite of passage and great adventure and about what lies ahead for their daughters and sons. I understand this. After all, as somebody once said to me

87

in a striking mixed metaphor: "The future is an uncharted sea full of potholes."

A newspaper columnist for the Olathe, Kansas, *Daily News*, David Chartrand, wrote recently about the life of college freshmen: "You'll know right off that this isn't high school anymore when you wake up and realize there is no one telling you: To get out of bed. To get back in bed. To turn off the television. To avoid strangers. To go to bed and I swear I am not kidding this time. . . . To help with the dishes. . . . To make your bed. . . . To eat your dinner. . . . To grow up. To stop growing up so fast." At Stanford we have no ambivalence about your growing up, nor will you hear the admonition to "avoid strangers." Quite to the contrary, you will be encouraged to go out of your way to meet strangers, to talk to strangers, to befriend strangers. The university and your fellow students offer you rich intellectual opportunities to explore and understand the many faces of diversity, here and abroad.

The Stanford college class of 1997 is exceedingly diverse by any measure of academic achievements and interests and artistic and athletic accomplishments. It is also diverse as expressed by common demographic yardsticks, even though some of these categories tend to be overly general. Indeed, they understate rather than capture your diversity.

Nonetheless, here are some figures from the demographic profile of the Stanford college class of 1997:

2 percent American Indian

5 percent foreign students, from thirty-seven different countries

9 percent African-American

10 percent Mexican-American

24 percent Asian-American

50 percent in that residual category called "white."

This last category, whatever the government may mean by it, refers, of course, only to students from the United States. The American students come from all fifty states and the District of Columbia.

Very few among you have graduated from a high school or lived in a community with such diversity. Not many will have had much personal experience of interacting with people of different ethnic, racial, and cultural backgrounds. As you cross bridges to meet strangers at Stanford, the going will sometimes be rough. That, however, is an inevitable part of the excitement that college offers you.

I should like to think through with you some of the issues that have become associated with diversity on college campuses. I do so because for you, our new students, these will be matters of great opportunity and challenge in the next few years. They are also, I am sure, of great interest, and sometimes concern, to you, the parents.

Last May I received a letter from the parents of a graduating college student from which I should like to quote the most important passages:

> Dear Dr. Casper:
>
> Our son, Andy, graduates from Stanford in a few weeks. He has enjoyed Stanford. . . . One of the reasons he elected to attend Stanford was the cultural richness of its student body. We recently received the Commencement schedule of events, and that concerns us. The following are some of the events shown:
>
> Chicano/Latino Graduation Ceremony
> Catholic Graduation mass and Reception
> Asian American Graduation Dinner
> Native American Graduation Dinner
> African American Graduation Program . . .

We should like your thoughts on the policy apparently being fostered of separating students along racial, ethnic and religious lines as evidenced by the Commencement schedule. We noticed the same atmosphere at Stanford four years ago when we enrolled our son. There were admissions receptions for African American, Asian, Native American, and Latino students at that time. Interestingly, there appear to be no receptions or campus groups for white Anglo Saxon students—and well there are not.

We applaud the efforts of Stanford to create a diverse academic atmosphere where various American cultures and ethnic groups can exchange ideas to enrich the whole academic environment. However, it appears that rather than creating an appreciation for diversity, Stanford is fostering separatism among its students. Isn't this the very thing Stanford is trying to eliminate in its admissions policies? Aren't we trying to create an amalgam of American culture rather than a cacophony?

I sometimes get fifty or more letters a day. They address many issues and express very different opinions—indeed, they often make dissonant, cacophonous points. My staff and I answer almost all of them. My reply to Andy's parents stressed that Stanford is certainly not pursuing a policy of fragmentation. I did point out, however, that maintaining a diverse academic community does require that students and their families feel at ease, especially at such festive occasions as the opening of the freshman year or commencement. Alas, the pressures of time did not permit me to address the last paragraph of the letter. In a way, what I should like to do today is belatedly to think aloud about the questions it raises as to the multiplicity of cultures represented on campus and the university's own culture. Especially, I am interested in the letter's last question: "Aren't we trying to create an amalgam of American culture rather than a cacophony?"

Let me begin by making the obvious point that students, like all other human beings, are individuals pursuing their individual aspirations, but they are also social beings. When they congregate with others on campus it does not necessarily mean that they are segregating themselves. Almost all of us have a tendency to hang out with people who are familiar, who share our background, who are "our own kind." We also have a tendency to form or join groups in order to accomplish some goals of ours. Any individual may associate with a range of different groups. The groups we belong to tend to maintain a group spirit. This is, incidentally, especially true as to the "group spirit" of American universities, Stanford included. The "Stanford spirit" was indeed one of the factors that enticed me to join the faculty last year. I trust you will embrace it quickly, because, whatever your differences may be, you have one thing in common—the choice of associating with Stanford.

Individual development often takes place through groups. Our Constitution recognizes this fact and need by protecting the freedom of association as part of our First Amendment rights. Those who critically characterize various campus groups as students "segregating" rather than as students "associating" choose to construe the phenomenon, to quote Stanford alumnus Woodrow Myers, as alienation, rather than as a means for exploring cultural identity—though the latter interpretation is frequently the most plausible one.

To be sure, the line between "congregation" and "segregation" is a fragile one. As you know, Stanford has a number of student residences that are designated as "theme houses," and some of these are ethnic theme houses. Stanford encourages interaction and guards against separatism by requiring that, in the case of the ethnic theme houses, no more than 50 percent of the residents may belong to the ethnic group that provides the "theme." This summer I talked with a student who during her freshman year had been assigned to one of these theme houses. She did indeed feel left out and ended up associating mostly with students from the "other" half. She liked neither the sense of exclusion nor the fact that, in this instance, "cross-cultural interaction" did not work. Cases like this are bound to occur because universities are not immune to social developments and tensions. I do, however, view it as the institutions' responsibility, and indeed as the responsibility of Stanford students, Stanford parents, Stanford alumni to do their utmost to minimize the chances for exclusion, even as we provide opportunities for identifying one's social heritage. I shall return to this matter later on.

The exploration of one's cultural identity has itself become a major theme in our country and our world. Experiences of social and political inequality have heightened emphasis on cultural differences. This in turn has led to what the Canadian philosopher Charles Taylor refers to as "the politics of recognition." Taking off from the concept of the equal dignity of all citizens, we are asked to recognize the unique identity of an individual or group, their distinctness from everyone else. The phenomenon is both a domestic and a global one. Cultural conflicts seem to characterize our world at an ever escalating speed: with devastating and heartbreaking consequences in the former Yugoslavia or in Somalia, or in South Africa, where a few weeks ago, a former Stanford student, Amy Biehl, died while contributing to the dismantling of apartheid.

More and more individuals seem to seek authenticity through some form of social identity, and this social identity is, to a large extent, tied up with a notion of social heritage as one's "culture." I think it is very important to realize that this fairly old-fashioned definition of culture as "social heritage" owes much of its contemporary currency to the undeniable fact that minorities, in the United States and in many other countries, are emerging from experiences of subordination or even submersion.

It is also the case that thinking in terms of "cultural wholes," in terms of distinct cultural identities, each more or less "complete," neglects the fact that there are myriad crossroads, bridges, and borderlands, especially in "a nation of immigrants" such as ours. To quote my Stanford colleague Renato Rosaldo:

We all cross such social boundaries in our daily lives. Even . . . the nuclear family, is cross-cut by differences of gender, generation, and age. Consider the disparate worlds one passes through in daily life, a round that includes home, eating out, working hours, adventures in consumer land, and a range of relationships, from intimacy to collegiality and friendship to enmity.

Radcliffe-Brown, the famous social anthropologist, spoke of culture as "the process by which a person acquires, from contacts with other persons or from such things as books or works of art, knowledge, skill, ideas, beliefs, tastes, sentiments." I, your president, am an immigrant, which, of course, you would never have guessed listening to my accent. I came to the United States from Germany in 1964, at age twenty-six, almost thirty years ago. When I moved initially to California, my "cultural identity" was certainly predominantly German—whatever that means. It is said easily but there are, after all, many different ways to be German or Indian or American or Italian. The adage "When in Rome, do as the Romans do!" does not deprive one of choices. In my case the matter of identity was further complicated by the fact that there was little to identify with for somebody who grew up among the devastations of World War II and the cultural uncertainties and ambivalences experienced by my generation in the wake of the horrors perpetrated by the Nazis. Since 1964 I have lived in the United States, and have had contacts with people in every part of the country, with books, architecture, art, music, even, believe it or not, football. I have acquired an American "cultural identity" intermingled with my original German and European identifications. For twenty-six years I lived in Chicago—as Saul Bellow has shown, a rather rich cultural challenge all by itself. I am now interacting with "the Stanford culture."

In addition, I have played many different roles, some of them on both sides of the Atlantic: the roles of son, student, husband, father, professor of constitutional law, dean, provost, president, friend, citizen—to mention but a few. The content and demands of these roles have been changing for me, as they have been changing for all of you. We have a difficult time indeed as we attempt to distinguish those traditional contents of a role that are worth retaining from those that should be discarded. Each of us has so many different roles with changing demands that most of the time it even seems beside the point to search for a role model—even a single specific role can be played in various ways, just like Hamlet. I think I have only one identity, but my identity, like yours, reflects myriad cultural influences and role expectations, which I have fused, adapted, integrated in my own individual way.

An acquaintance of mine who had come to the United States through various way stations from eastern Europe, once said: "I would go back to where I came from, if I hadn't come from so many places." Each one of us is actually "multicultural," has come from "so many places." Each one of us will become even more multicultural as we befriend more "strangers." Indeed, it is the opportunity to meet "strangers" that adds special pleasures to life, especially at a university.

So, were Andy's parents right when they rhetorically asked: "Aren't we trying to create an amalgam of American culture rather than a cacophony?" It may surprise you to hear that I do not think that they were right. There is a great difference between a distillation that you have freely produced yourselves and one ordained by the university in accordance with its social engineering schemes. "We," in this case Stanford University, have no particular mandate to create a "culture," be it an "amalgam" or a highly differentiated one. Each one of you will develop your own version of cultural identity, will become a person. Your fellow students and your faculty and members of the staff, and therefore, in a manner of speaking, "the" university, will obviously make many contributions to your cultural formation. All of this will happen whether any of it is intended or not. As T. S. Eliot has said: "Culture is the one thing that we cannot deliberately aim at. It is the product of a variety of more or less harmonious activities, each pursued for its own sake."

Culture is a highly dynamic concept. No culture is ever frozen, not even those that are completely isolated. One's social heritage does not come neatly packaged in an ice cube that can be thawed for reference and use. Nor are we frozen into a particular culture. But it is not for the university in its institutional role to tell you to blend in or to remain separate, to embrace an "amalgam" or to reject it. Whether the United States is best understood as a "melting pot" or a "mosaic" you will decide. However, neither of these metaphors of rather dubious analytic quality is a normative component of Stanford's "mission" statement. It is not our goal to mold you in a particular way. What is university policy is "a commitment to actively learning about and interacting with a variety of different people." If we at the university were not committed to interactive pluralism, education would become impossible.

Of course, this does not mean that the university should ignore the fact that different students have different interests and wants and that the institution's diversity creates acculturation difficulties for individuals that need to be attended to with care. The university is an institution dedicated to the search to know, the search to know of each member in her or his individual capacity. You were admitted to Stanford as individuals, not in groups. No university can thrive unless each member is accepted as an individual and can speak and will be listened to without regard to labels and stereotypes. While the university has no right to tell you who you should become, with what groups to associate or not to associate, university citizenship entails the obligation to accept every individual member of the community as a contributor to the search to know. In a university nobody has the right to deny another person's right to speak his or her mind, to speak plainly, without concealment and to the point. In a university discussion your first question in response to an argument must never be "Does she belong to the right group?" Instead, the only criterion is "Does she have a valid argument?" An argument must not be judged by whether the speaker is male or female, black or white, American or foreign.

I could end here and thus avoid some additional problems. However, let me retain you for a few moments more. If what I just said suggests to you that I see the university as by and large neutral territory where cultures clash, interact, adapt, and change while the institution itself is committed to cultural relativism, with no ideas and values of its own, you would be quite wrong. A university has a culture, an identity of its own. Its identity is tied to its work. Its work, as I said, consists of the search to know. The search to know is carried out by critical analysis, according to standards of evidence that themselves are subject to examination and reexamination. They cannot be set by a political diktat. Thomas Jefferson spoke of freedom as "the first born daughter of science."

What I like to refer to as the "republic of learning" is committed to, I quote the philosopher Martha Nussbaum, "the Stoic ideal of the kosmou polites, or 'citizen of the entire world,' that is, the ideal of being a person who can argue intelligently about the most important matters with human beings the world over, not being shut out of such debate by narrowness or prejudice." As Randolph Bourne wrote during the First World War:

> A college where such a spirit is possible even to the smallest degree, has within itself the seeds of this international intellectual world of the future. It suggests that the contribution of America will be an intellectual internationalism which goes far beyond the mere exchange of scientific ideas and discoveries and the cold recording of facts. It will be an intellectual sympathy which is not satisfied until it has got at the heart of the different cultural expressions, and felt as they feel. It may have immense preferences, but it will make understanding and not indignation its end. Such a sympathy will unite and not divide.

The work of the university is universal by aspiration and character. The "republic of learning" reaches from Florence to Stanford, from Stanford to Kyoto, from Kyoto to Santiago, from Santiago to Moscow—all places, incidentally, where Stanford has a presence, as it has in Paris, Berlin, and Oxford. I know few universities that are better positioned than Stanford on the Pacific Rim to be at the center of this "republic of learning."

The "republic of learning" has values that it prizes above all others: freedom (not just academic freedom), nondiscrimination (you will be heard regardless of your sex, race, ethnicity, religion), and equality of opportunity. It is not a mere coincidence that these are also the values, if at times distorted or forgotten, of our country.

Nor is it a coincidence that the culture envisioned by Jane and Leland Stanford, as put forward in the 1885 Founding Grant for the University, comprised "teaching the blessings of liberty regulated by law, and inculcating love and reverence for the great principles of government as derived from the inalienable rights of man to life, liberty, and the pursuit of happiness." These purposes are not a coincidence, because studies cannot blossom and minds cannot move unless these rights prevail, unless the wind of freedom blows, not only at the university but also in the wider society. "The wind of freedom blows"—Die Luft der Freiheit weht—is the motto that appears in the seal of the president of Stanford University. It was chosen by Stanford's first president, David Starr Jordan. In a symbolic expression of the fact that the "republic of learning" knows no national or cultural boundaries, President Jordan employed the motto that can be traced to the humanist Ulrich von Hutten in German rather than English.

In June, I wrote a letter to all Stanford alumni in which I discussed undergraduate education. The letter triggered responses from hundreds of our former students. Among them was one from Walter Pendergrass in Portland, Oregon. Mr. Pendergrass told me how, after the first train ride of his life, he arrived in September of 1942, "a very unsophisticated, shy and apprehensive seventeen and a half year old." He concluded his reminiscences by writing, and I quote:

> So what do I remember from yesterday and hope for today, and tomorrow? A Stanford where there is a warm and honest welcoming to all; where there is exciting, challenging and rewarding opportunity to learn academically and to be a positive part of the world; and where there is opportunity to reflect that we are but a very small part of a very big picture.

This is one summary of what I hope for you, the Stanford college class of 1997. It is also, in a way, a summary of what I have said this afternoon, if in a somewhat more elaborate and complicated way. It is an expression of the "Stanford spirit." Once again, Stanford extends a "warm and honest" welcome to all of you and to your families and wishes you an "exciting, challenging, and rewarding opportunity to learn" so that you may experience the pleasures that come from studies blossoming and minds moving.

Context

The early 1990s was probably the decade during which multiculturalism and identity politics were most prominent in the United States in general and on American campuses in particular. When I came to Stanford in 1992, I was ill equipped to deal with some of these issues. While, to be sure, demographic diversity of students and faculty had been big issues at the University of Chicago, "multiculturalism" was not a predominant concept. I obviously had followed the general discussions in the country, but I did not participate in them. I was unprepared in another sense. Since I did so deeply believe in the university as an integrated center of teaching, learning, and research, the multicultural positioning of ethnic groups in the competition for influence and resources at universities, and its disaggregating aspects, made me very uncomfortable.

Since a 1989 *Final Report of the University Committee on Minority Issues* (subtitled "Building a Multiracial, Multicultural University Community"), Stanford had mobilized along a multicultural agenda with "vision statements," standards, self-studies, and annual review panels. By the turn of the decade (and when I came to Stanford), "multiculturalism" had become a highly charged preoccupation for some faculty, staff, and students at Stanford.

The university's vision statement on multicultural diversity read: "The University has a vision of Institutionalizing [*sic!*] the achievement of multiculturalism. The ultimate objective is to attain numerical diversity and evolve to the more difficult accomplishment of interactive pluralism."

At one level, this was probably mostly about pressing for more affirmative action and a multiracial, multiethnic campus community that was inclusive. The operative noun, however, was "multiculturalism"—an exceedingly vague term that changed its meaning with the context in which it was used. While "diversity" suggests a university whose members come from many different backgrounds—racial, ethnic, social, intellectual, geographic, economic—the problem with the noun "multiculturalism" is that it suggests a comprehensive ideology. The referent is to "many cultures," with some connotation of separateness. Indeed, the 1989 *Final Report*'s recommendations had emphasized "ethnic *group* or *community* identity in student life," ethnic programs, and ethnic studies. In 1990, Stanford had established an Office for Multicultural Development in the Office of the President that took the place of a university office that had focused on affirmative action.

By the time I arrived at Stanford, the implementation of the multicultural agenda (in itself not very clear) had been affected by the university's budget deficits that had been caused primarily by the indirect cost disputes with the federal government.

Andy's parents, in the letter from which I quoted, asked the (rhetorical) question: "Aren't we trying to create an amalgam of American culture rather than a cacophony?" American culture, whether an "amalgam" or not, is, of course, very strong. Indeed, some, like Kwame Anthony Appiah, find "the broad cultural homogeneity of America more striking than its much-vaunted variety." However, the multicultural disputes were not about the reality of American life, they were not empirical, but they were normative. At one end of the political spectrum were those who saw the future of the United States, like, in their view, its past, as assimilation. At the other end were those who, to quote Appiah again, "now insist that they are profoundly shaped by the groups to which they belong, that their social identity—their membership in these groups—is central to who they are. Moreover, they go on to pursue what the Canadian philosopher Charles Taylor calls a 'politics of recognition': they ask the rest of us to acknowledge publicly their 'authentic' identities."

The public debate suffered greatly from the fact that terms with significantly different denotations and connotations, such as "diversity," "identity," and "multiculturalism," often were used in almost interchangeable ways and, furthermore, were linked to affirmative action that now was meant to apply not only to employment and admissions but, through the politics of recognition and respect, to the use of resources for enhancing the cultural content of identities, especially on campus.

The ideal of authentic identity came to combine two different quests: On the one hand, it reflected the Enlightenment emphasis on the individual, on the other hand, it turned the search for authenticity into a search for authentic social identity.

Charles Taylor saw the eighteenth-century German philosopher Johann Gottfried Herder as the major articulator of this combination:

> Herder put forward the idea that each of us has an original way of being human: each person has his or her own "measure." This idea has burrowed very deep into modern consciousness. It is a new idea. Before the late eighteenth century, no one thought that the differences

between human beings had this kind of moral significance. There is a certain way of being human that is *my*
way. I am called upon to live my life in this way, and not in
imitation of anyone else's life. But this notion gives a new
importance to being true to myself. If I am not, I miss the
point of my life; I miss what being human is for *me*. . . .

Herder applied his conception of originality at two
levels, not only to the individual person among other
persons, but also to the culture-bearing people among
other peoples.

In my remarks to the freshman class and their parents, I clearly embraced individualism without pausing to consider the question what
the limits of individualism might be, especially, whether a polity can
survive, when the human pursuit is primarily about "*my*" way. The
question I did raise was that of social identity in cultural terms,
warning students against a simplistic view of social heritage and taking a critical view of "social engineering" by the university. I was
worried that multicultural university policies might contribute to
fragmentation. I was also worried that multiculturalism was increasing peer pressure on students to define themselves in terms of race
and ethnicity. For me, it had always been an article of faith that the
university could never do its job unless all members actively interacted, "crossed bridges."

However, as my talk makes clear, I also felt a need to push
back against often-vociferous criticism that Stanford, with its ethnic
theme houses, had allowed segregation. Three theme houses for
African-Americans, Asian-Americans, and Chicanos/Latinos were
created in the late 1960s and the early 1970s by the then new Office
of Residential Education. One for Native Americans followed in
1988. The theme houses (with a total of about three hundred beds,
or roughly 4 percent of undergraduate housing) were not exclusive
to the ethnicity providing the theme and were developed "as places
where minority and White students can participate together in a

residential education program focusing on minority culture; and as places where minority students can choose to live with many others of their ethnic group." The theme houses were supported by large majorities among minority students (though less so by Asian-Americans) and remained a subject of considerable controversy among students of primarily European or, as they say in California, "Anglo" descent. They were anathema to many, though by no means all, alumni.

Had I been at Stanford when the theme houses were contemplated, I would probably have opposed them. I did not undertake to have them reconsidered. As is so frequently the case when precedents have been established, efforts to overturn these precedents are likely to result in opposition that would be even stronger than the original demand for the precedent. I thus decided not to reopen the issue.

Postscript I

My speech "Concerning Culture and Cultures" was delivered on September 23, 1993. I gave a slightly different version of it in a nationally broadcast talk to the Commonwealth Club of San Francisco in March 1994.

In the course of the academic year 1993–94, Stanford and I faced a considerable number of complex diversity issues, at all levels of the university.

The first one was the promulgation of a new policy on sexual harassment. Stanford was still employing a policy that had been adopted in 1981. Drafts of a new policy had been languishing for three years, creating what I considered to be an insupportable situation. After intensive consultations, I was able, on October 6, to put into effect a policy that had the unanimous endorsement of the Faculty Senate. The new policy emphasized the informal resolutions of complaints, strengthened language on confidentiality, and provided for trained sexual harassment advisers.

In November, the Provost's Committee on the Recruitment and Retention of Women, chaired by Professor Myra Strober, a labor economist, submitted its report. The picture drawn by the committee was not an encouraging one, as is indicated by the report's opening paragraph: "In the last twenty-five years, American colleges and universities, including Stanford, have increased the number and percentage of women on their faculties. For example, between 1974–75 and 1992–93, Stanford increased the percentage of women faculty by almost 9 percentage points (from 7 percent to almost 16 percent) and the percentage of tenured women faculty by 7 percentage points (from 4 percent to 11 percent). However, *43 percent of Stanford departments still have no tenured women. Moreover, during the last 5 years, in departments where there were new faculty hired, almost 40 percent hired no women*" [emphasis in the original]. The report also showed that, from a comparative perspective, Stanford ranked very low indeed among peer institutions.

The document received a detailed and vigorous review in the Faculty Senate. Its recommendations led to some progress in increasing the representation of women in faculty and leadership positions, and in improving the climate for women on campus. The rate of progress, however, remained slow, in spite of many, including personal, efforts in this regard. I shall return to the issue in a later chapter.

In the course of the year, I decided to confront the Western Association of Schools and Colleges (WASC), Stanford's accrediting agency, over a "Statement on Diversity," which I considered inappropriate for an academic accreditation organization, amounting as it did to interference with the autonomy of universities. That battle, very much of my own choosing, left me in a delicate and awkward position. I had to convince the Stanford community that, in good faith, I could assert support for diversity in education and, at the same time, lead the fight against the active promotion of diversity as an accreditation standard imposed by an outside agency. While I received the unanimous support of the Faculty Senate, I was eventually defeated by the WASC bureaucracy. I shall deal with this and other accreditation issues more fully in the next chapter.

In the 1993–94 fiscal year, Stanford faced major concerns of a financial nature. After cuts of $43 million in the university's unrestricted operating budget in the preceding fiscal years, Provost Condoleezza Rice and I had come to the conclusion that we needed to achieve an additional $20 million in reductions. We tried to protect academic programs to the largest extent possible and asked administrative units to achieve additional 15–30 percent budget savings over three years, beginning with the 1994–95 fiscal year.

Furthermore, we had to make provisions to proceed with $158 million in vital earthquake repairs, reconstruction, and seismic strengthening. Finally, we needed to reconceptualize and restructure university budgets by taking into account both the unrestricted and the restricted revenues and expenditures of all parts of the university on a consolidated basis. Condi Rice was an extraordinarily effective manager of the university budget, and we were actually able to balance the budget by 1995. However, the year 1993–94 was wrenching for virtually all people and all parts of the university.

The vice provost for student affairs, Mary Edmonds, was faced with the task of cutting $1 million and did not exempt any of her operations, including the ethnic community centers, from being reviewed. In that, she had, as a matter of principle, the provost's and my full backing, though our position increased tensions when it was interpreted as a lack of support for the centers. There were four such ethnic community centers, with a total budget of almost $600,000. In the end, their allocation was not reduced but instead increased by $100,000 a year for two years for "both graduate and undergraduate recruitment planning and cultural and educational programming" for the larger campus community.

While the ethnic centers were generally uneasy about Condi Rice and me, high tension developed over Mary Edmonds's decision to eliminate the position of associate dean for development in her office and assign the responsibility to the university Office of Development. The position had been found to be unnecessary, including by its incumbent, Cecilia Burciaga, who had originally come to Stanford in 1974 as assistant to the president for Chicano affairs and who was the highest-ranking Chicana administrator at Stanford. She and her husband, an artist, were also the resident fellows at Casa Zapata, the Chicano/Latino theme house. While a substantial number of Chicanos saw her as a role model, in this third, most difficult, budget reduction phase, we were not any longer able simply to assign senior staff to a position different from the one that had been eliminated. After Stanford, Burciaga joined the founding team for the California State University at Monterey Bay.

There is a Stanford tradition of rowdy Sunday Night Flicks. On May 1, in honor of Cinco de Mayo, Chicano students showed a 10-minute video by the United Farm Workers called *No Grapes* before the evening's feature, *Mrs. Doubtfire*. The video was about the effect of pesticides on farmworkers. Some members of the audience protested and began to shout slurs, such as "Beaners go home."

On May 4, a Wednesday, Chicano students decided on a protest that had been in the making for several weeks in support of four major demands: another high-level job for Burciaga, a Chicano studies major, a university-wide ban on grapes, and a community center for the nearby city of East Palo Alto. Four Chicanas went on a fast that lasted three days.

The protest and the fast took place in the Main Quad. According to the *Stanford Daily*, at its high point, on its second day, it attracted some 250 students. The protest ended after Condi Rice and I agreed to issue a statement that three committees would be appointed to examine three (of the four) issues raised by the Chicano students: a grape boycott on campus, a Chicano studies program, and enhanced collaborations with East Palo Alto. We referred the demands for Chicano studies (plus Asian-American studies, which we had added to the list) to the dean of the School of Humanities and Sciences as the venue for considering new programs in the social sciences. We did not grant any request with respect to Burciaga.

On Saturday morning, there was a "handshake ceremony" and a signing of the statement that the provost and I had issued.

Condi Rice and I walked over to the tents where a number of chairs had been prepared. There were two empty chairs for us, and there were four chairs for the hunger strikers. As we reached the circle, the approximately sixty assembled students chanted in Spanish, "Grapes, No—Chicano Studies, Yes."

I went over to shake the hands of the hunger strikers, and all but one accepted that handshake. Condi Rice and I then sat down. The chants went on for a few minutes. When they stopped, I said:

> I know that your strike was importantly about respect—respect that the provost and I always had for you even though some of you may have felt otherwise. We do respect you and your sense of commitment. I have no respect for those who, under cover of darkness, shout slurs. We now have a positive basis on which to move forward. I should like to remind all of us that universities are very fragile institutions (as we have again learned in the last few days) because they ultimately are based solely on the power of argument and reason—though clearly, our feelings also play an important role.

Feelings prevailed a few days later, on May 12, when Asian-American students disrupted a meeting of the Faculty Senate to demand that a motion be tabled for the immediate creation of an Asian-American studies program. A sophomore exclaimed: "This struggle has been going on for almost twenty-five years; of course, we are frustrated. We keep being told to talk to someone else, but there comes a point where students' patience starts to fade and they want to take things into their own hands."

After twenty minutes, the Senate chair, Patricia Jones, a professor of biology, adjourned the meeting. It so happened that that afternoon I was to give my annual State of the University Address to the Academic Council. Thus we moved from one auditorium to another and, without interference, I spoke about "The University in a Political Context." This will be the text for the next chapter.

Postscript II

1. When it rains it pours. In the early morning hours of May 16, 1994, *Gay Liberation,* a statue by George Segal, was attacked by seven varsity athletes. The sculpture, located on Lomita Mall, is composed of four white painted bronze figures (two men and two women) and two benches. The two men are standing, one placing an arm on the shoulder of the other. The two women are sitting on one of the benches, lightly touching. The sculpture was a second cast of statues originally commissioned for, and at the time rejected by, New York City and Los Angeles. When the sculpture was installed in 1984, it was immediately and severely assailed by vandals. A second attack followed a few years later. This was the third attack. The statues were spray-painted black. The Stanford police, who are deputy sheriffs exercising their powers under an agreement between the university and the Santa Clara County sheriff, made arrests and reported the cases to the Office of the Santa Clara County District Attorney. It is long-standing Stanford policy that the university will not interfere with police and district attorney once they have initiated a case. In this instance, arrestees were eventually convicted and sentenced to probation and community service, while on a parallel track, also in accord with long-standing practice, the university disciplined the students. I was subjected to the usual array of letters taking me to task for acting too forcefully or for not acting forcefully enough.

2. With respect to a university-wide ban on grapes, the university, in 1988, had responded to a demand for a grape boycott in support of farmworkers and improvements in their working conditions by giving members of each student residence a choice whether to serve the fruit or not. In 1994, students repeated the call for a university-wide ban because of the use of pesticides by the growers.

The boycott of California table grapes had been a prominent part of the agenda for the United Farm Workers of America under the leadership of César Chávez and was ended only in 2000. In 1995, after a year of inquiry into the issue and a detailed and probing thirty-eight-page report by a committee under the chairmanship of Luis Fraga, a political science professor and director of the Stanford Center for Chicano Research, I concluded that the called-for university-wide boycott of grapes was not justified (though, for pragmatic reasons, we did not overturn the 1988 policy).

In a joint statement, Provost Rice and I said:

> We understand . . . that the grape issue is of significance to members of the Chicano community, an essential and valued part of Stanford University. Stanford is committed to access to higher education for all and has worked hard to diversify its student body, faculty and staff. That increasing diversity makes it more important than ever that the university not take political stands on the ground that a particular group, or a portion of a group, feels strongly about a specific cause. Doing so would cast the president and officers of Stanford as judges of the relative moral and political weight of the positions of the university's many voices. Taken to its extreme, the university would become a patchwork of limitations and regulations based on the political causes of different groups. That we cannot permit. . . .
>
> The university is foremost a place for teaching, learning, and research. Its fundamental purpose is not the resolution of political issues—no matter how pressing or how important. Only when such issues directly affect the core teaching and research mission or other important institutional interests should Stanford's officers attempt to bring the university's weight to bear on the political process.

For the most part, the delicate task of balancing the myriad interests and beliefs of Americans, and of collectively resolving social issues, lies elsewhere—in our democratic institutions. There, as citizens, Stanford students, faculty, and staff influence the course of events through the exercise of individual rights and responsibilities.

I had, of course, in my inaugural speech, quoted Harry Kalven to the effect that a university "cannot take collective action on the issues of the day without endangering the conditions for its existence and effectiveness." For years, I had also worried about the sapping of political life that followed from conveniently targeting universities for the failings of governments and politicians.

3. On the issue of ethnic studies, the appropriate bodies of the School of Humanities and Sciences, under the leadership of Dean John Shoven, and the university decided in 1996, after a two-year examination, to establish an interdisciplinary Center for Comparative Studies in Race and Ethnicity that affiliated existing programs (the university had had a Program in African and African-American Studies since 1969), and that established four new tracks based on interdisciplinary and comparative approaches to understanding the complexities of race and ethnicity and how they have shaped the course of history and the social fabric of the contemporary world. The center offers majors and minors in four areas: comparative studies, Asian-American studies, Chicano studies, and Native American studies. The Taube Center for Jewish Studies is also affiliated and has a research division.

4. In June of 1994, "an event of seismic proportions in the world of education" (*New York Times*) occurred at Stanford when the Faculty Senate voted in favor of reintroducing the failing grade (it had been abolished more than twenty years earlier) and generally tightened grading and course requirements. The Senate acted in accordance with recommendations that had been issued by its

Committee on Academic Appraisal and Achievement, chaired by Gail Mahood, professor of geological and environmental sciences. I am mentioning this development to underscore that, all along, we were attending to general academic concerns and needs. The most important undergraduate educational reform was still in the making. The Commission on Undergraduate Education that I had appointed in October 1993, under the chairmanship of historian James Sheehan, was about to issue its report in September. The report opened with the statement: "The most important aim of undergraduate education is to involve students in [the search for knowledge], where teaching and learning, instruction and research, the communication and discovery of knowledge are combined in a single enterprise."

6.

The University
in a Political Context

State of the University Address, Kresge Auditorium

MAY 12, 1994

Text

As you know, last Wednesday, a group of Chicano students began a protest on the Quad, including four Chicanas who chose to engage in a fast. They, like all of us, feel the uncertainty and stress that inevitably accompany times of contracting, rather than expanding, resources. The provost and I suspended most other business and met with the students several times over three days. We have agreed to the establishment of committees to examine their concerns in depth and make recommendations.

It was crucial—*crucial*—to the provost and me that the university's constituted processes for making decisions be followed. Practically any issue is open to discussion at the university. When the provost and I can be responsive, we will be. But we cannot work for Stanford's future in an environment dominated by the politics of ultimatum. I should like to state in the most unambiguous terms that, without faculty and student and staff support in this fundamental respect, we cannot perform our tasks. As we have again learned in the last few days, universities are very fragile institutions. If we short-cut argument and reason, we abandon the essence of the university. If universities make their substantive decisions for political, rather than academic, reasons, they have no particular claim to untrammeled existence.

I said to the students last Saturday that we do respect them. I also said that we have no respect for those who, under cover of darkness, shout slurs. On this point, the Chicano students and the provost and I have been in complete agreement from the start: The actions of some members of the audience during the showing of the film *No Grapes* at the May 1 ASSU Sunday Flicks were unacceptable. Let me reiterate that I was appalled to hear that some people made remarks that were at best stupid and at worst racist. Such behavior has no place whatsoever at Stanford.

I also repeat what I said in my inaugural address and have repeated many times since: "No university can thrive unless each member is accepted as an autonomous individual and can speak and will be listened to without regard to labels and stereotypes." This is the sine qua non of all universities, and not just because universities are arguably the most diverse communities in America.

We must manage to maintain Stanford as a place whose common denominator is to protect the openness, the rigor, the seriousness of our work in education and research—as what I like to call a *noncommunitarian community*. My friend Edward Levi once characterized how we must do that. He wrote:

> It requires clarity, intellectual rigor, humility, and honesty. It requires commitment and considerable energy. It requires that we ask questions, not only of others but of ourselves. It requires that we not only examine the beliefs of others but those newly acquired doctrines which we are all prone to believe because they are held by the group we favor, or are the cherished aspirations that come to us

in the middle of the night and which we are certain cannot be wrong. Habits of thought and searching intellectual honesty must be acquired and forever renewed.

Stanford must let nothing weaken its commitment to the power of
reason.
[A number of report items are omitted from the reproduction of
the text.]

As Senator Stanford had hoped when he accepted David Starr
Jordan's recommendation on a motto for this university, the winds
of freedom generally have blown over Stanford and American higher
education, both private and public. While the United States Constitution does not specifically protect academic freedom, on the whole,
the First Amendment guarantee of free speech—and, even more
important, the civic and political culture supporting it and higher
education—have kept government out of "the four essential freedoms" of a university cited in 1957 by Justice Frankfurter in his
famous concurrence in *Sweezy v. New Hampshire*. They are a university's freedom "to determine for itself on academic grounds *who* may
teach, *what* may be taught, *how* it shall be taught, and *who* may be
admitted to study."

To be sure, at times, such as the McCarthy period, these values were put to a stern test. However, in a worldwide comparison,
there can be little question that the United States may be proud of
the freedom from government its universities have enjoyed as to
Frankfurter's core freedoms.

There has been a sense in America that academic freedom
serves not only those who are its direct beneficiaries—universities
and their faculties and students—but also society. As Justice Frankfurter wrote in *Sweezy:*

Progress in the natural sciences is not remotely confined
to findings made in the laboratory. Insights into the mys-
teries of nature are born of hypothesis and speculation.
The more so is this true in the pursuit of understanding

in the groping endeavors of what are called the social sciences, the concern of which is man and society. . . . For society's good—if understanding be an essential need of society—inquiries into these problems, speculations about them, stimulation in others of reflection upon them, must be left as unfettered as possible. Political power must abstain from intrusion into this activity of freedom, pursued in the interest of wise government and the people's well-being, except for reasons that are exigent and obviously compelling.

I think it is fair to say that these exhortations are no more than exactly that—exhortations, urgent appeals. As little as universities are ivory towers are they legally autonomous. Whatever constitutional protections universities and their members enjoy are those of every other citizen, no more, no less. There are implications for every citizen in the rising tide of government intervention in the form of regulation. As a university faculty, we have a special responsibility to concern ourselves with government-university interactions.

One of my highest priorities since coming here a year and a half ago has been to engage my faculty colleagues, our students, the staff, the trustees, and the university's alumni and friends in a review of our institutional priorities—particularly our curriculum and policies related to research and teaching. I wanted our focus to be an internal one. What kind of institution are we? What should we be? What should we do? How should we do it? In short, I wanted to concern myself with the objects of Justice Frankfurter's "four essential freedoms."

However, all too often my attention has been drawn from internal considerations and diverted to issues involving government. I have long known that contemporary research universities, including the private ones, are heavily dependent on government in many, mostly inevitable, ways and from many jurisdictions. From my new vantage point, I am concerned that the very character of universities could be transformed—and their contributions reduced.

Let me discuss two aspects of government-university interactions today that cause me concern: the serious side effects of direct regulation of essential activities and efforts to extend regulation into fundamental educational processes.

On the first issue—the side effects of direct regulation—many university research activities cannot be conducted unless they comply with government regulations. Research involving animals, human subjects, radioactive materials, DNA, contagious diseases, and what we now define as hazardous substances is subject to various government prescriptions and proscriptions.

We have accommodated this seemingly inexorable expansion and simply added the expenses to our cost of doing business. At present, however, we find ourselves increasingly subject to regulatory processes that begin seriously to interfere with the very nature of the academic enterprise, especially on the research side. Let me recount, for example, the recent regulatory activity in the State of California with respect to the use, storage, and disposal of hazardous wastes at Stanford.

At Stanford, more than four thousand faculty, staff, and students work with chemicals, and the resulting waste, in one way or another. Research involving thousands of chemicals is conducted in roughly seven hundred locations in schools and departments throughout the campus.

California has promulgated hazardous waste regulations to protect human health and safety, preserve the environment, minimize waste, and prevent pollution. These rules, however, were developed with large-scale manufacturing processes and industrial settings in mind. And that was a wise decision by the state because 99.99 percent of all hazardous chemical waste comes from manufacturing and industrial processes; less than one one-hundredth of a percent comes from university laboratories.

Officials freely admit that the development of the regulations did not take into account the nature and organization of universities. The result is agreement between the university and the state on objectives and outcomes—safe practices, sound management of waste, environmental protection—and sharp disagreements on paperwork, administration, and organizational requirements.

Take, for example, labeling. Research and teaching at Stanford produce about twenty-five thousand small containers of chemical waste annually—most of them smaller than a glass of water. State regulators require that each of those containers be labeled with a special label itemizing six specific pieces of information, even if the chemical is in its originally labeled container provided by the manufacturer. An error on any one of these items is a violation. Furthermore, if a state inspector finds a container mislabeled in laboratory A on the west side of the campus and on a subsequent visit finds that another container is so mislabeled in laboratory B on the east side of the campus, Stanford can be considered "recalcitrant" because "repeat" violations have occurred. Labeling fines range from $100 to $10,000 per violation. A 1 percent error rate, therefore, could result in annual fines of $25,000 to $2.5 million.

In one actual incident, a conscientious graduate student at Stanford put the wrong date on a bottle because his calendar watch was off by a single day, and by chance a state inspector that day noted the resulting labeling violation. The student's supervising faculty member, a distinguished member of our chemistry department, Paul Wender, wrote a memorandum on the incident to our Environmental Safety Office. Professor Wender commented:

> I would invite . . . the inspector to meet with this individual and better understand how serious he and others are about compliance and how inspections that focus on such human errors and *not on more pressing issues of safety* serve only a destructive purpose. . . . We have very little time these days to do much science because it seems

that every week there is a new issue, many of a reasonable nature but far too many of which simply do not address safety. . . . If we continue to focus on non-problems, we will not achieve what should be the objective of our safety programs and legislation, i.e., to create a safer environment. Instead we will discourage compliance and drive our educational and research system into the ground.

Unhappily, I report to you that our most serious disagreements with the state are not over labeling. I merely use this example because it can be readily understood, and it illustrates the regulatory attitude we are dealing with. Nevertheless, we can live with labeling—if that were our only problem. But it is not.

Far more important to us are complicated issues of authority over laboratory practices, the definition of laboratory and associated work spaces, the requirements for supervision and storage of chemicals, the length of time substances can remain in a laboratory, when a substance becomes a waste, when containers can be reused, what training documentation is required for different job classifications and for students, and other important issues.

We seek agreement with the state on interpretations of existing regulations. Real environmental protection is not at issue, nor is compliance with the law. Stanford understands and agrees with the importance of both of these objectives. At bottom, our dispute is not about whether these activities should be regulated; it is over the state's rigid interpretation of regulations designed for industrial processes and its insistence on applying those to university laboratories. It is the country that will suffer if the research enterprise is smothered by red tape.

My argument is that seemingly "neutral" rules and their serious side effects are beginning to make the research enterprise extraordinarily difficult for reasons that are not, to use Justice Frankfurter's formulation, exigent and obviously compelling. "It matters little," Frankfurter wrote, "whether such intervention occurs avowedly or through action that inevitably tends to check the ardor and fearlessness of scholars, qualities at once so fragile and so indispensable for fruitful academic labor." Transaction costs can extinguish scientific ardor as effectively as the Inquisition, never mind that many regulators are behaving as if they were the Inquisition.

A second area of concern regarding government and universities has to do with recent efforts by the government and regional accrediting associations to intrude on educational processes at colleges and universities. Here we are talking no longer about side effects but about avowed intervention. This country's higher education system, although clearly not without its share of faults, remains the best in the world. As my colleague Steven B. Sample, president of the University of Southern California, recently wrote in a letter to the *Los Angeles Times:*

> No one I've ever met believes this extraordinary level of excellence is due to increasingly intrusive accrediting bodies or increasingly burdensome regulation. Rather the excellence of our colleges and universities is attributed to their freedom to be different from each other—to their ability to take risks and chart their own destinies in a highly competitive environment.

In 1992, Congress added several new sections to the 1965 Higher Education Act intended to address increasing fraud and abuse in student loan programs. This abuse is largely found in short-term proprietary trade schools, not in the vast majority of higher education institutions. One of the new sections added to the act required each state to establish a State Postsecondary Review Entity—the acronym is SPRE; you had better learn it—to investigate problem institutions according to specific standards.

Early versions of proposed regulations to implement this part of the Higher Education Act, however, appeared to apply new standards of control to *all* institutions, not just those that fail to meet the tests of sound management established by the underlying law.

These regulations would have increased *both* federal and state control over institutions that administer student aid programs properly, even though such institutions were never the target of the law.

To the credit of the secretary of education, final regulations recently promulgated have removed troubling ambiguities and limited the scope of authority of the SPREs. But the SPREs will be required to set certain standards for institutions subject to review, and the entry of the government into these matters carries with it the potential for expansion and unwise intrusions.

Another section of the Higher Education Act provides for greater control over accrediting associations. Accrediting associations are nominally voluntary, nongovernmental bodies that provide a seal of approval for institutions ranging from trade schools through research universities. I say "nominally" voluntary, because this seal of approval is taken by the secretary of education as a determining factor in the eligibility of an institution and its students for federal programs, such as educational grants and guaranteed student loans.

In an effort to make the regional accrediting associations themselves more accountable, new sections of the Higher Education Act require twelve standards that accrediting bodies must use in their evaluation process. These standards cover such areas as curricula, faculty policies, recruitment and admissions practices, tuition and fees, and measures of student achievement. In short, government is contemplating to intrude on "the four freedoms" of a university—"to determine for itself on academic grounds who may teach, what may be taught, how it shall be taught, and who may be admitted to study."

The six regional accrediting associations are certainly aware of these developments. In California we are under the jurisdiction of the Western Association of Schools and Colleges (WASC), which issued a proposal entitled "The Future of Self-Regulation." The very title of the report is disturbing, marking a shift from accreditation—WASC's traditional role—to regulation.

The argument is that teaching is the one common denominator of all colleges and universities, and that there is widespread public dissatisfaction with our performance in this area. Therefore, WASC should guard the public's interest by ensuring that institutions measure teaching effectiveness, hire and promote faculty on the basis of their abilities as teachers, dedicate appropriate financial resources to teaching, and require their governing boards to involve themselves directly in the review of educational quality.

Any university president who objects to this kind of regulation is in a delicate position. We stand to be accused of not valuing teaching and of favoring research, or of not wanting to be accountable for our institutions or our faculty, or—to use that all-purpose insult of the day—of being arrogant. But we cannot let the debate be shifted in this way. The presidents of all the universities with which Stanford competes—and we are very competitive—are committed to providing the best possible education for undergraduates. And on many campuses, including, of course, ours, there are large-scale reviews of undergraduate programs under way. We are voluntarily taking a fresh look at the educational component of our mission. We need to do so to remain competitive.

On the matter of assessing educational outcomes, no matter how attractive the notion is, some basic facts must be considered. There is very little evidence that the outcome of an undergraduate education can be measured in any rigorous way on a broad scale. General achievement tests are too crude a measure to assess vast differences in the preparation students bring to college, the differences in colleges themselves, or the differences in programs within colleges and universities. Students attend our institutions for a variety of reasons and with a variety of expectations, have a variety of experiences while in school, and leave with a broad range of outcomes. The value of an education is not measured at a single point in time. Indeed, as many of our alumni attest, appreciation for education often increases many years after graduation. And, as someone who has been engaged for decades in discussions with college and professional school alumni, let me assure you that "the public" whose interest the would-be regulators would like to protect has not arrived at any agreement whatsoever as to what precisely it wants its universities to provide.

The best investigation into teaching effectiveness that I know of is being done at Harvard by Professor Richard J. Light in the Harvard Assessment Seminars. These are an intensive series of discussions, surveys, interviews, and evaluations that focus on the experiences of particular groups of students in particular programs and that are designed to lead to specific policy recommendations that can be acted upon by the faculty and the administration.

In the second of a series of reports on this work, Light writes:

> [We] quickly and unanimously agreed on one unalterable principle. Our explorations, the sample surveys, the in-depth interviews, the evaluations of curricula, *must all be first-class science.* This principle may seem obvious. But we often remind ourselves that without good science, we will accomplish little.

The kinds of investigation WASC proposes do not meet the criteria of first-class science. WASC suggests, for example, that we measure how much our students use the library as a way of determining whether they are spending sufficient time studying. Or, that we analyze patterns of enrollment to see what choices our students are making about their studies. Or worse still, many of its recommendations deal with issues of process and governance: How are faculty hired and promoted? How are financial decisions made? What is the role of governing boards? None of these, arguably, provides any direct evidence about learning outcomes. As a group, however, these processes represent the very essence of self-governance and institutional autonomy.

It serves no purpose to require institutions to gather costly yet trivial statistics as a substitute for real evidence. In fact, if we were forced to take on the expense of satisfying WASC guidelines in this area, we would have fewer resources to devote to thoughtful and careful evaluations of our educational programs.

The WASC proposal will now be debated among the membership, and I hope that the outcome will be a significantly modified policy that respects the difficulty inherent in trying to measure effectiveness. There is hope.

Whether there is hope in the larger arena of amendments to the Higher Education Act is less clear. The final regulations promulgated by the Department of Education are a vast improvement over earlier proposed versions. We are grateful for the responsiveness of the secretary and his staff to an outpouring of critical comment from colleges and universities.

Nonetheless, the final, joint, product of the new laws and regulations is a greatly expanded oversight structure for higher education that draws states into new policing roles as federal deputies, substantially federalizes an already flawed accreditation system, and arrogates to federal officials significant decision-making authority over the four freedoms of a university.

These trends require our attention. We should not allow ourselves to slip unintentionally toward a "ministry of education" that imposes standards and academic policies for every institution in the country. To do so would be to risk bringing an end to the breadth, diversity, and quality of our system of higher education. And let me say with all the authority conferred upon me by my accent: let us not "Europeanize" American higher education.

I have not intended these observations and reflections on two quite different aspects of the government-university relationship to be a comprehensive statement. Also, it would be churlish of me to speak so long about government and the university and only discuss troublesome matters. On balance, we have to conclude that the government has been a generous and, for many decades, benign patron. As former President Lyman pointed out some years ago, it has generally refrained from interfering with internal operations at universities, isolated exceptions notwithstanding. For the past several decades, it has funded institutions, students, and merit-based research with salutary effects on learning, science, and society as a whole.

My concern—and sometimes my alarm—is that we may be seeing a shift away from the interests of "wise government" spoken of by Justice Frankfurter.

I worry most of all that we may take universities for granted. It might be assumed that they can absorb increasing political demands and regulation, and the accompanying increase in operating costs, while remaining unaffected in their quality, their vitality, and their ability to contribute to society as they have so magnificently done. If I had only one message to leave with you, it would be that you not permit that profound misconception to gain currency.

And let me repeat what I said earlier: If we want to claim our four freedoms, we must make our decisions on academic grounds.

Context

On September 10, 1964, I arrived in Berkeley to begin my appointment as an assistant professor of political science at the University of California. On that same day, an anonymous former student wrote in a Berkeley student newspaper that undergraduates needed to organize and "split the campus wide open" for fierce and thoroughgoing rebellion. Within days, the Berkeley student revolt, soon to be known as the Free Speech Movement, began. The triggering event was the university administration's ill-considered prohibition of tables for political advocacy and solicitations on a twenty-six-foot strip of university property at the University and Bancroft Avenues entrance to the campus. In the following weeks, dramatic confrontations between students and police took place, and Mario Savio emerged as the leader of the Free Speech Movement. On December 3, in the early morning hours, police arrested some eight hundred students who had occupied Sproul Hall, the administration building. I was teaching a class on the concept of law for about one hundred undergraduates during the fall quarter. At least a quarter of my class ended up in jail. Faculty and others collected money for bail, and the next day five thousand students gathered for a demonstration in front of Sproul Hall. Much of my introduction to academic life in the United States was taken up with emergency meetings to address the issues.

Mainly for professional reasons, but in part due to the relentless politicization of Berkeley, I accepted an offer from the University of Chicago in 1966. Turmoil followed at, among others, Columbia, Cornell, Harvard, Stanford, Chicago, and Kent State. The 1968 May protests in Paris were the most significant international manifestation of what had begun at Berkeley four years earlier.

As concerns Stanford, I may quote President Richard Lyman's ironically understated summary in his book on the campus unrest from 1966 to 1972. "Our troubles were not as widely noticed as those at Columbia, Berkeley, Harvard, and Cornell. People are surprised to hear that we had a half-dozen major cases of arson, suffered significant damage to campus buildings, principally in the form of broken windows, and during the notorious 'Cambodia-Spring' of 1970 had to summon police to the campus repeatedly to end sit-ins or deal with other disruptions; dozens of police and students were hurt. One Stanford president had his office burned, with a loss of a lifetime's mementos; his successor was forced to resign after just nineteen months in office for his inability to cope with the uproar."

After some prior sit-ins, the University of Chicago saw the occupation of its administration building, in 1969, by more than four hundred students who protested the university's decision not to reappoint Marlene Dixon, an assistant professor of sociology. The occupation lasted for two weeks while university officers and staff worked elsewhere and the faculty met almost daily. After the police brutality at the 1968 Democratic National Convention in Chicago, Edward Levi, the president of the university, was determined not to call the police. Instead, the university waited the students out and proceeded with university disciplinary committees against many of them. Expulsions from the university and suspensions resulted. Law students, with assistance from faculty, including me, organized the students' defense.

Throughout my academic life, I have seen universities as wonderful but also fragile institutions. They are vulnerable not only to coercion and disruption but also to political influence (both inside and out), to the influence of money, to the temptations of growth and publicity, to bureaucratic suffocation. They also are vulnerable because of the sheer lack of understanding in a broad public of what universities are about and how they work. For me, the important question always has been how the university can distinguish itself from other societal, especially political, institutions. In addition to teaching, learning, and research, the essence—of even the "multiversity" that the contemporary university has become—has to be decision making on academic grounds.

The "political context" of my 1994 state of the university address to the Academic Council included the Stanford protests the background for which I provided in the preceding chapter. My speech then turned to state regulation, and the text concerning the then pending case with the California Environmental Protection Agency is, I believe, self-explanatory.

In the end, the California EPA chose to interpret existing regulations in ways that bore no rational relationship to the reality of the university setting, and imposed $460,000 in fines, $235,000 in state administrative costs, and $300,000 in contributions to private environmental groups. Perhaps worse, it imposed expensive and unnecessary bureaucratic requirements on us for the future. Real environmental protection was not at issue, nor was compliance with the law. The dispute was not about whether these activities should be regulated; it was over the state's rigid interpretation of regulations designed for industrial processes and its insistence on applying those to university laboratories. The state sanctions were far from trivial and had to be paid from the unrestricted revenue of the university—that is, from funds that could have gone to financial aid and other academic purposes.

One of the most disturbing aspects of the state sanctions was the exaction of $300,000 from the university for redistribution to private environmental groups of the state's choosing. This is the modern administrative state at its discretionary worst. To use formulations of Richard Epstein from a slightly different context: broad agency delegation leaves the amounts and objectives of redistribution at the mercy of political pressures. And, for all practical purposes, there is no judicial recourse.

There is also no recourse when it comes to accreditation, the second regulatory subject that I addressed in my state of the university address.

College accreditation in the United States has acquired a Byzantine and distinctly corporatist character. More or less compulsory and monopolistic organizations of colleges and universities ("associations") are recognized by the government for purposes of accreditation and to obtain compliance with government policies. Eligibility for various federal programs, especially financial assistance to students, depends on an institution's accreditation. The associational leaders intermediate between what they believe to be (or, more realistically, what they believe "should be") the interests of their members and the government. It did not start out this way.

What began, at the end of the nineteenth century, with truly voluntary associations of schools and colleges that attempted to provide standards became a more complex system in the first half of the twentieth century, as quality assurance through peer recognition was sought additionally for professional and other specialized schools. The current behemoth began to emerge when the federal government entered the picture with the GI Bill of 1944 and its successors.

It is the usual story. The federal government, of course, has no constitutionally granted jurisdiction over education, but it has money—initially for veterans and then for student aid more generally—and it has great needs to assure against fraud. In 1952,

Congress required the secretary of education to publish a list of accreditation agencies that were recognized by the secretary. The Higher Education Act of 1965, a major piece of "Great Society" legislation, provided broad-based financial aid for students in public and private institutions and also strengthened accreditation oversight. Since the Higher Education Act, by its own terms, must be reauthorized every few years, Congress has used these occasions to increase the role of the federal government in higher education to root out fraud and establish some quality assurance.

The government's approach is a model of corporatism: the secretary of education (advised by the National Advisory Committee on Institutional Quality and Integrity) accredits the accreditors, which in turn accredit educational institutions. The accreditors are "voluntary," "private," "nongovernmental" associations.

In parallel, there exists an umbrella organization made up of three thousand institutional members that also scrutinizes and certifies accreditors: the Council for Higher Education Accreditation. Following in the footsteps of a number of predecessors, CHEA was formed in 1996 and views itself as "a primary voice for voluntary accreditation and quality assurance to the U.S. Congress and the U.S. Department of Education." The whole scheme is referred to as "self-regulation" (the "self" supposedly being colleges and universities). The more "self-regulation" they get, the less self-governance is enjoyed by universities.

In 1992, the year I became president of Stanford, the Higher Education Act dramatically expanded the reach of accreditation. The final regulations under Section 496 required that accreditors address the quality of an institution in the following areas:

(i) Success with respect to student achievement in relation to the institution's mission, including, as appropriate, consideration of course completion, State licensing examination, and job placement rates.
(ii) Curricula.

(iii) Faculty.

(iv) Facilities, equipment, and supplies.

(v) Fiscal and administrative capacity as appropriate to the specified scale of operations.

(vi) Student support services.

(vii) Recruiting and admissions practices, academic calendars, catalogs, publications, grading, and advertising.

(viii) Measures of program length and the objectives of the degrees or credentials offered.

(ix) Record of student complaints received by, or available to, the agency.

(x) Record of compliance with the institution's program responsibilities under Title IV of the Act, based on the most recent student loan default rate data provided by the Secretary, the results of financial or compliance audits, program reviews, and any other information that the Secretary may provide to the agency.

On top of all this, the regulation gave a recognized accrediting agency free hand to "establish any additional accreditation standards it deems appropriate."

The Western Association of Schools and Colleges had first formulated a "diversity" standard in 1988. About 1992, it began to work on a "Statement on Diversity" that was supposed to make the standard meaningful by identifying "three vital and related dimensions: (1) representation; (2) the nature of the campus community; and (3) the impact of group membership on both individual development and the content of academic scholarship and study." The statement went on for nine pages detailing these considerations. It was adopted unanimously on February 23, 1994, by the commission running WASC. While the institutional members of the "association" had no vote, the overwhelming majority of WASC institutions (including the University of California campuses) expressed support for the statement. As the late Martin Trow, a professor of public policy at Berkeley, put it: "Academics, and especially administrators, are extremely sensitive about saying anything that might be construed as unresponsive to the diversity of America, and especially of California." Only seventeen colleges indicated their opposition. In addition to Stanford, this group included Caltech, Claremont McKenna, Mills, Pepperdine, Saint Thomas Aquinas, and USC. In my opposition to the statement I was supported by a unanimous Stanford Faculty Senate.

While the leadership of the University of California did not align itself with us, the Academic Council of the Academic Senate of the University of California had opposed WASC intrusion in 1992, and Martin Trow, its former chairman, submitted comments to WASC in 1993 in which he forcefully asserted that the policy statement was nothing other than a political position that claims moral superiority to alternatives:

> The pretensions to consensus should be seen to be hollow, mostly trading on what is a broadly shared view that welcomes diverse parts of the population into the academy. But this sense of breadth of inclusion in no way justifies a regional accrediting agency, charged primarily with the modest task of determining whether an institution is a genuine college and not a secondary school or a fraud, setting forth doctrines about what are correct attitudes toward "diversity" in higher education, together with quite detailed criteria with respect to the treatment of group differences in admissions, appointments and the curriculum.

Martin Trow had previously encountered this particular set of issues in 1991–92, when he served as chair of the national advisory committee on accreditation to Lamar Alexander, then the secretary of education. The Commission on Higher Education of the Middle

States Association had threatened the accreditation of Westminster Theological Seminary and Baruch College for insufficient diversity. Alexander, who came to his cabinet post directly from the presidency of the University of Tennessee, on academic and religious freedom grounds, withheld action on the Middle States' petition for renewal of its recognition as an accreditor. In response to the secretary's criticism, the Middle States Association "clarified its original goals" by stating that no adverse accreditation action would be taken solely on the basis of diversity. The association was then rerecognized.

By the time WASC adopted its statement on diversity, the Higher Education Act had been amended and a new secretary, who came from a governor's position rather than higher education, was in office. Even before its action on diversity, WASC circulated a second policy draft ("Report on the Future of Self-Regulation") that was even more troubling than the diversity statement. It called for a complete overhaul of the standards by which the institutions were to be accredited. It argued that learning outcomes should be the focus of accreditation, though many of its specific recommendations dealt with issues of process and governance: How are faculty hired and promoted? How are financial decisions made? How are governing boards engaged in the educational process?

In a letter, eighteen other university and college presidents and I said:

> The very language and tone of the report is startling. We have understood the purpose and expertise of WASC to be in accrediting institutions, not in regulating them. It is dangerous to presume that these functions are equivalent. Second, the report portrays our institutions, many of which are private, as enjoying a special "grant of freedom" that may soon be revoked. We find this an odd interpretation of the independence that we enjoy in an open and democratic society.

WASC's position that higher education institutions enjoy a special grant of freedom that may soon be revoked is, I believe, indicative of what has been happening in the field of accreditation. The "private" accreditation bureaucracies probably are staffed by many true believers. However, they also are staffed by people who are essentially performing a governmental function and who therefore worry about government and want "to forestall the worst." Many contemporary standardizing accreditation policies might be considered a form of voluntary "Gleichschaltung," or "bringing into line" (akin to the government-imposed Gleichschaltung of German universities after 1933).

Postscript I

In the years immediately following Stanford's dispute with WASC, I played a minor role on the national accreditation scene, which was in considerable turmoil. After the 1993 dissolution of the Council of Postsecondary Accreditation (COPA), I joined a Presidents Work Group of twenty-five members that was to develop a proposal for an organization or system "to coordinate accreditation and recognize both institutional and specialized accrediting bodies." Within the work group I advocated an "issue-oriented clearinghouse, not a governing body." In particular, I was opposed to a new organization taking on the function of recognizing accreditors. I thought that any independent recognition of accrediting agencies stood to be either redundant or in conflict with the federal process. To my eyes, there was no point in setting up a system that mirrored the federal one, especially in light of the extensive regulations issued by the Department of Education. Corporatism makes it even harder to hold the government accountable since it exercises control indirectly. However, in the discussions of the Presidents Work Group, I was part of a tiny minority.

The most notable victory for antiregulation forces was the nonfunding by the House of Representatives of the State Postsecondary

Review Entities (the infamous SPREs to which I referred in my state of the university address). They were eliminated from the Higher Education Act altogether in the 1998 reauthorization.

While I lost on the recognition issue in the Presidents Work Group, the Council for Higher Education Accreditation (CHEA) that was formed is, by comparison with its predecessors, institutionally based and therefore in some, if attenuated, way accountable to its three thousand accredited member colleges and universities. Indeed, it has been willing to be critical of developments, especially Secretary Margaret Spelling's 2005–6 Commission on the Future of Higher Education, which pushed for further federalization of accreditation.

To quote Judith Eaton, the CEHA president:

> By "federalizing" accreditation, the government takes on some of the academic decision making that has traditionally been carried out by faculty and academic administrators. For example, the federal government, since 2008, has had at least some legal or regulatory authority over how a credit hour is defined, transfer of credit, distance learning, and how enrollment growth is managed, among other areas. U.S. Department of Education (USDE) guidelines for accreditors extend to student-learning outcomes, general education, and curriculum— all arguably the province of faculty.

The State Department maintains a website on "Accreditation in the United States." On this website it says: "The United States has no Federal Ministry of Education or other centralized authority exercising single national control over postsecondary educational institutions in this country. The States assume varying degrees of control over education, but, in general, institutions of higher education are permitted to operate with considerable independence and autonomy."

I am not so sure. Probably ministries of education in other developed democracies, at least de facto, do not exercise much more control than is now the case for the Department of Education and the other federal government agencies that possess regulatory powers over higher education. It is ironic, indeed, that much of the rest of the world is examining the governance models that made American higher education great at the very moment when American policy makers seem to be abandoning them.

The list of issues concerning the role of tertiary education in modern societies is never ending. There are many legitimate controversies. Myriad choices have to be made in order to determine strategies that are appropriate for ambitious and competitive institutions. The question is: Who makes these choices? It is hard to believe that, on the whole, legislatures, governmental bureaucracies, and accreditors can choose more wisely than the institutions themselves, provided those institutions have appropriate leadership and high levels of robust debate. Recent research comparing European universities among themselves and with American public universities shows that the more autonomous and the more competitive universities are, the more compelling their strategic choices will be.

I return to the Western Association of Schools and Colleges. In line with the fashionable emphasis on "outcomes," WASC, on November 3, 2011, adopted a new "graduation proficiency" standard for undergraduate degrees that requires their institutions "to demonstrate that their graduates have achieved the institution's stated level of proficiency at least in the following five areas: written and oral communication, quantitative skills, critical thinking, and information literacy." At least two of these "proficiencies" were to be externally validated.

In commenting on the standard, Stanford's provost, John Etchemendy, wrote in early January 2012:

> It is our belief that the Commission's Graduation Proficiency requirement oversteps the bounds of its authority as an accrediting body by usurping academic decisions—in particular, about the nature and character of General Education requirements—that are the legitimate

domain of the colleges and universities awarding the degrees. Moreover, the standard reflects a naïve and potentially harmful view of the aims of undergraduate education and threatens to both obscure and distort the missions of institutions forced to conform to the standard.

As I write this, WASC has suspended implementation of its requirements "until further consultation is conducted."

My successor as president, John Hennessy, shall have the last word. In a 2010 "Open Letter to the Senior Accrediting Commission of the Western Association of Schools and Colleges" he wrote:

Some 15 years ago, Stanford was among a number of institutions whose leaders expressed serious dissatisfaction with WASC. They argued that the Commission and its staff were out of touch with the members, arrogant in their use of authority and ideologically driven in the development of new accreditation standards. To its credit, WASC instituted some welcome reforms and entered a period of experimentation and innovation. However, it appears that history is repeating itself and it is time once again to call for change.

Postscript II

David Horowitz, a conservative writer, in the early 2000s began promoting an Academic Bill of Rights aimed primarily at protecting students from what he saw as the political bias of faculty members (stressing the fact that Democrats outweigh Republicans on most campuses). In 2005, the Academic Bill of Rights began to become of concern to some colleges, and the then president of Foothill College, Bernadine Chuck Fong, asked me to address the underlying issues. The following text has been adapted from a speech I gave at the college.

Let me turn to the academic freedom of faculty members, in particular. I begin with Arthur Lovejoy, whose definition in the 1930 *Encyclopedia of the Social Sciences* is succinct.

> Academic freedom is the freedom of the teacher or research worker in higher institutions of learning to investigate and discuss the problem of his science and to express his conclusions whether through publication or in the instruction of students, without interference from political or ecclesiastical authority, or from the administration officials of the institution in which he is employed unless his methods are found by qualified bodies of his own profession to be clearly incompetent or contrary to professional ethics.

I submit that this definition covers classroom teaching and the administration of examinations within the clearly articulated goals of a faculty member's course, the conduct of research, the publication of research. Having said that, these activities must be neither "clearly incompetent" nor clearly "contrary to professional ethics." Alas, both incompetence and violations of professional ethics can be found in colleges and universities. One of the worst of such violations is the use of the lectern for the propagation of one's own political preferences. It is the sin against the holy spirit of learning.

However, who would know better than a law professor how uncertain the line between the scholarly and the political often is. This uncertainty is the reason why the judgment over matters of this kind is committed to professional bodies rather than political or societal authorities; this is the reason why universities have a large measure of autonomy. Academic freedom, to a large extent, is a procedural right to protect the individual from being disqualified for unqualified reasons.

Let me provide a fairly stark illustration from Justice Frankfurter's opinion in *Sweezy v. New Hampshire* (1957). Sweezy was a Marxist economist who had been invited to give a guest lecture at the University of New Hampshire. This led to a government inquiry at which Sweezy refused to answer certain questions. I quote from the opinion.

> The questions that petitioner refused to answer regarding the university lecture, the third given by him in three years at the invitation of the faculty for humanities, were:
>
> "What was the subject of your lecture?"
>
> "Didn't you tell the class at the University of New Hampshire on Monday, March 22, 1954, that Socialism was inevitable in this country?"
>
> "Did you advocate Marxism at that time?"
>
> "Did you express the opinion, or did you make the statement at that time that Socialism was inevitable in America?"
>
> "Did you in this last lecture on March 22 or in any of the former lectures espouse the theory of dialectical materialism?"
>
> "I have in the file here a statement from a person who attended your class, and I will read it in part because I don't want you to think I am just fishing. 'His talk this time was on the inevitability of the Socialist program. It was a glossed-over interpretation of the materialist dialectic.'"

Justice Frankfurter classified governmental intrusion into the intellectual life of a university as "grave harm." He said: "These pages need not be burdened with proof, based on the testimony of a cloud of impressive witnesses, of the dependence of a free society on free universities. This means the exclusion of governmental intervention in the intellectual life of a university. It matters little whether such intervention occurs avowedly or through action that inevitably tends to check the ardor and fearlessness of scholars, qualities at once so fragile and so indispensable for fruitful academic labor."

The point about the *Academic Bill of Rights* that is presently discussed is not that its values are wrong. I have examined it repeatedly and, as a matter of principles and values, found little to object to. For instance, how can one possibly object to a rule that says: "Students will be graded solely on the basis of their reasoned answers and appropriate knowledge of the subjects and the disciplines they study, not on the basis of their political or religious beliefs." I cannot imagine many, or for that matter, any college teachers who would want or see it otherwise. Or, another example: "Exposing students to the spectrum of significant scholarly viewpoints on the subjects examined in their courses is a major responsibility of faculty. Faculty will not use their courses for the purpose of political, ideological, religious or anti-religious indoctrination." What makes one wary is the potential that the formal adoption of such "bill of rights" by legislatures or public governing boards has for the further legalization of college life.

In the American context anything called a "bill of rights" suggests legal disputes, suggests formal appellate procedures, even litigation. Either rights come with legal remedies, or these are attached later. Admittedly, the bills introduced in state legislatures so far, and the "Sense of Congress" resolution that has been pending in the House of Representatives, either are weak on enforcement provisions or lack them altogether. I wish I could have confidence that, if enacted, they will not become new reference points for imaginative lawyers.

My presidential encounters with lawyers, both government and private, frequently reminded me of my close friend and former Chicago colleague, the late constitutional scholar Philip Kurland. He was much disenchanted with what you might call an "anything goes" approach in law. A Kurland faculty club roundtable exchange with George Stigler, the Nobel economist, has become legendary. Stigler, at lunch, began a sentence by opining, "No lawyer would . . ." Whereupon Phil Kurland interrupted him impatiently, saying: "Stop right there. There is no way you can finish that sentence!"

The fact of the matter is that most issues of academic freedom tend to be immensely complex and subtle, deeply embedded in a culture of academic discourse. I do not believe for one moment that we would be better off with some sort of additional regulation. On the whole, we should assume that the academic marketplace, with its competition for students and faculty, will support the right institutional values. Among those values, I should like to say emphatically, are effective internal grievance procedures for both faculty and students.

For one grievance, however, there is no remedy. Any remedy would be worse than the situation complained about. A recent study that has received a lot of attention purports to show that liberals and Democrats by far outnumber conservatives and Republicans on college faculties. I have not seen the actual study, but I am perfectly prepared to believe the result. George Stigler, the self-described "conservative professor of economics," said, back in the sixties of the last century, that, as concerns economics departments, he considered it likely "that it is harder for a conservative (and also for a socialist) of given scientific ability to get appointed at most American universities than for a man whose views fall in the New Deal–Great Society range."

The *Academic Bill of Rights,* in a very cautious way, tries to address this kind of issue in its first article. I quote:

> All faculty shall be hired, fired, promoted, and granted tenure on the basis of their competence and appropriate knowledge in the field of their expertise and, in the humanities, the social sciences, and the arts, with a view toward fostering a plurality of methodologies and perspectives. No faculty shall be hired or fired or denied promotion or tenure on the basis of his or her political or religious beliefs.

The last sentence makes it clear that politics must not provide the *basis* for faculty appointments, and the preceding one suggests no more than keeping in view the fostering of a plurality of methodologies and perspectives. I, for one, agree with that goal. The work of the university is work that cannot be done unless it is continuously reconsidered and supported afresh by faculty and students. Such reconsideration is highly unlikely if there is only one dominant way of thinking.

In 1966, the same George Stigler quoted just above, in a letter to the chair of the Stanford Board of Trustees, responded to the question whether the trustees should push the appointment of conservative professors. He wrote: "If we allowed influential groups to dictate faculty appointments, a university would turn into a squabbling, partisan debating society."

In the last paragraph of the letter he said:

> The Trustees have a responsibility of their own to see
> that the faculty is as honestly chosen as mortal schemes
> allow. This could not be achieved by direct interven-
> tion in appointments, even if the academic world
> accepted the intervention. It can be sought only by
> communicating to the President and senior adminis-
> trators of the university an unremitting insistence
> upon the sovereign role of scientific ability in faculty
> appointments—a creed which must in turn be inces-
> santly emphasized to the faculty.

Universities and colleges are human institutions made
up of faculty and students that need to be committed to
an academic ethic. There is also no question that we need
to remind ourselves of the norms that should govern our
actions frequently because our schemes are only "mortal."

On the other hand, to return to Justice Frankfurter,
society should not engage in actions that "tend to check
the ardor and fearlessness of scholars, qualities at once so
fragile and so indispensable for fruitful academic labor."

The good news is that as fragile as fearlessness may
be, it is also a personal quality that we can foster in ourselves.

7.

Affirmative Action

OCTOBER 4, 1995

Text

Keeping open an avenue
whereby the deserving and exceptional
may rise through their own efforts

With increasing frequency, students, faculty, trustees, alumni, and others have asked where Stanford should be on affirmative action. I determined several months ago to express my own views on the subject to the Stanford community at the first Faculty Senate meeting of the fall. Affirmative action involves some of the most difficult and complex issues in our society. Reasonable people differ on what it means, has meant, or ought to mean. In the hope that it will facilitate further examination and discussion, I offer my full statement here to the senators, and all of Stanford, in advance of the October 12 Senate meeting.

Government-mandated affirmative action began with President Lyndon Johnson's Executive Order 11246 of 1965. Affirmative action requirements applicable to the employment decisions of federal contractors, including universities, were substantially reinforced and extended under President Nixon. Most regulations originate

141

with the executive branch rather than Congress, and require out-reach, plans, goals, and timetables. State regulations also come into play. Some affirmative action—for instance, in college admissions—is voluntary in the sense of not being mandated by government.

Affirmative action does not require, and does not mean, quotas or preferment of unqualified over qualified individuals. Indeed, such preferment may violate antidiscrimination laws. Affirmative action is based on the judgment that a policy of true equal opportunity needs to create opportunities for members of historically underrepresented groups to be drawn into various walks of life from which they might otherwise be shut out. Barriers continue to exist in society, and therefore affirmative action asks us to cast our net more widely to broaden the competition and to engage in more active efforts for locating and recruiting applicants.

Of course, the very act of broadening the competition means that more candidates will seek, and be considered for, the same finite number of admissions places or employment openings, and the competition for them will therefore be more intense. It would be hypocritical to suggest that affirmative action, even without quotas, does not diminish the opportunities for some who, in the past, might have benefited from a narrower casting of nets or narrower definitions of merit.

The terms "merit" and "qualified" occasionally are used as if they were self-defining. Merit, however, ordinarily depends on many qualities of an individual and on judgments about how their combination might further the tasks of a university, government agency, or any other organization. Still, I repeat: Affirmative action does not justify admitting, hiring, or promoting those who are not well qualified for the work ahead of them.

For about thirty years, debate about affirmative action has been constant, though only occasionally very heated. In 1995, the discussion has become more intense and much louder. It is not sufficient to explain this phenomenon in terms of electoral politics. The politicians are responding to views and opinions whose forceful expression has triggered, and been triggered by, plans for a referendum in California. The California Civil Rights Initiative, as presently worded, would prohibit using "race, sex, color, ethnicity or national origin as a criterion for either discriminating against or granting preferential treatment" to anyone in public schools, employment, or contracting. The initiative is not—at least not directly—aimed at private institutions such as Stanford University.

It is often unclear why a given public controversy erupts at a particular moment. I am not an expert on social movements, and my hunches may or may not have some basis in fact. To me it seems that a confluence of various trends has led to the present crescendo concerning affirmative action.

1. The traditions of our country emphasize the individual person and individual autonomy rather than group membership. The Fourteenth Amendment of the United States Constitution was primarily aimed at the unequal treatment of individuals on account of race. Affirmative action makes group membership a salient characteristic of an individual. This defining element has left many Americans uneasy, including some supporters of affirmative action.

2. Because affirmative action has conferred legal status on group membership, many are worried about a balkanization of our society. They are especially concerned about the possibility that some separatist forms of multiculturalism are incompatible with the desire of maintaining a more open and more stable country. While American law mostly forgoes quotas, there is a suspicion that plans, goals, and timetables represent a "quota mentality."

3. Claims for the benefits of affirmative action have been proliferating. They have thus undercut the original rationale for affirmative action that flowed not

exclusively, but primarily, from the historical grievances of African-Americans. Groups that have been
the victims of a multiplicity of social, cultural, religious, and economic traditions and institutions advance claims that raise complex questions about the
responsibilities and competencies of government.

4. Our country, for the past thirty years, has been going
through vast demographic, economic, and social trans-
formations that seem to bring into question many, if
not all, values that once dominated. Also, economic
uncertainties a few decades ago did not seem to have
the comprehensive reach that, for instance, characterizes present-day "downsizing." As only too many
Americans know, downsizing may leave the unskilled,
skilled, and highly skilled of all age groups alike sud-
denly without jobs. In this setting, education becomes
even more crucial than it has always been. Thus getting
into a good school that has only a limited number of
places is an urgent desire of many students and their
families. They worry about whether they will receive
fair consideration in competitions in which, at Stanford, for example, less than 20 percent of the already
self-selected applicants to the freshmen class are offered
admission.

I should like to address further the specific subject of college
admissions at Stanford. To the extent to which I deal with questions
concerning underlying principles, much of what I should like to say
also applies to, or at least has implications for, employment at Stanford. I am making these comments against the background of the
national debate about affirmative action. However, I am restricting
myself to what Stanford is doing and what, in my view, it should be
doing. I have emphasized in the past, and I repeat now, that Stanford

University is a private institution that has, and should have, considerable freedom in the pursuit of its educational goals and ideals.

Let me begin by speaking about what Stanford has stood for since its founding. When Leland Stanford and his wife, Jane, lost their fifteen-year-old only child, Leland Jr., in 1884, they decided to use their wealth to do something for "other people's" sons and daughters. This sentiment led to the founding of our university.

In a 1902 address, which formally amended the Founding Grant, Jane Stanford stressed that the moving spirit of the founders was "love of humanity and a desire to render the greatest possible service to mankind." I quote: "The University was accordingly designed for the betterment of mankind morally, spiritually, intellectually, physically, and materially. The public at large, and not alone the comparatively few students who can attend the University, are the chief and ultimate beneficiaries of the foundation." The university's "chief object" was to be "the instruction of students with a view to producing leaders and educators in every field of science and industry."

The university's initial policy of not charging tuition was adopted, I again quote Jane Stanford, to "resist the tendency to the stratification of society, by keeping open an avenue whereby the deserving and exceptional may rise through their own efforts from the lowest to the highest station in life. A spirit of equality must accordingly be maintained within the University." I point out that Stanford admitted women when many of its peers would not even have considered the possibility.

The means that Jane and Leland Stanford chose to implement their lofty goal "to promote the public welfare" was to found, endow, and have maintained "a University of high degree." The quality of the university was the sine qua non for the pursuit of the more general ends. Nowadays, we would go beyond seeking a university merely of high degree and instead refer to achieving and keeping a university of the highest degree.

This evocation of our institutional purposes is helpful in reminding us that it would be exceedingly narrow-minded to assume that the pursuit of the university as envisioned in the founding documents calls for a one-dimensional approach in choosing those to whom we give the opportunity to study at Stanford. As we look for the leaders of tomorrow, if all we considered were capacities measurable on a scale, without taking into consideration other aspects of being "deserving and exceptional," we would be betraying the Founders. We would be betraying the Founders if we disregarded their stated concern about "the tendency to the stratification of society."

In the early years of Stanford, to gain admission as an undergraduate, you could choose between taking the university's entrance examination or presenting certificates from your school that showed that your grades were a set percentage higher than the lowest passing grade at the school. In short, you had to demonstrate the ability to do the work of the university.

Under David Starr Jordan's "radical plan," the only specifically prescribed subject was English, and Stanford, ahead of its time, considerably liberalized the other admission prerequisites. This allowed a wider group of students to qualify for admission to Stanford than under more orthodox systems, in which universities overdetermined the required preparatory subjects and thus limited the pool of students to the graduates of certain secondary schools. Most students entered Stanford by certification rather than examination, and, in 1911, the university abolished its own examinations, relying on the College Entrance Examination Board instead.

Under the influence of Lewis Terman, in 1920, Stanford additionally began to require an aptitude test. The Stanford test eventually was supplanted by the SAT. The Committee on Admissions used a ten-point system in which school record and aptitude test received three points each, while four points were reserved for the committee's judgment regarding "the student's personal qualities, general promise and so on." Since 1950, the university has been looking for evidence of a strong academic record in high school, the results of standardized tests, and three recommendation letters to confirm qualities of intellectual vitality, character, citizenship, and initiative.

These generally applicable considerations were supplemented by the Faculty Senate in 1986 with a more detailed set of Criteria for Undergraduate Admissions. According to the principles laid down in 1986, "The primary criterion for admission is academic excellence" as demonstrated by scholastic performance, scores on standardized national tests, documented perseverance and attainment in activities outside the classroom, the personal statement, and high school recommendations.

There are no restrictive quotas of any kind, and admissions are decided without regard to an applicant's economic resources. Stanford seeks undergraduates of varied ethnic, social, cultural, and economic backgrounds whose talents, achievements, and characters suit them for leadership. In the case of every person admitted, there has been a judgment that the applicant is "deserving and exceptional."

A few categories of applicants—certain ethnic minorities, legacies, and athletes—receive special consideration provided they meet these requirements. Children of Stanford alumni receive preference among applicants of approximately equal qualifications, as do children of eligible faculty and staff. Furthermore, Stanford is committed to a substantial presence of African-Americans, Mexican-Americans, and Native Americans in the undergraduate student body. Finally, the Department of Athletics may designate outstanding athletes for special attention. The dean of undergraduate admission and financial aid has final authority over all admissions.

All applicants receive careful consideration, and the admissions review takes individual circumstances of the applicant into consideration. These efforts aim at a class characterized by diversity in terms of academic interests, artistic and athletic accomplishments, leadership qualities, and ethnic and social backgrounds. Why should we look for such diversity? The main goals are two. First, we want a rich educational environment to challenge our students. Students learn much from one another. Second, we want to be faithful to our task to educate leaders for a diverse and complex society—a society that will, we hope, overcome the undue tendencies toward stratification. This cannot be done unless the country's demographic diversity finds a presence on campus.

We do not admit minorities to do them a favor. We want students from a variety of backgrounds to help fulfill our educational responsibilities, not, to my mind, to address the effects of historic discrimination, although that might be a result. University admissions offices are not set up to sit in judgment on what injustices society should compensate for and who should pay the price. Furthermore, who possesses the wisdom and insight for the task? Admissions decisions, on the basis of an applicant's demonstrated achievements, should be forward-looking. We must not admit some and thereby exclude others because we arrogate to ourselves the power to sort out who owes what to whom.

How an individual applicant has dealt with disadvantage obviously is relevant to assessments of capability and resilience. However, I am extremely wary of any admissions process in which economic and social disadvantage (including dysfunctional home environments) become categorical criteria to be formally weighed in decisions about whom to admit as a student. In order to survive as a sane society, we should not create incentives for ever more people to think in terms of victimhood or to play the role of victims, or to suggest that one must be disadvantaged to be given serious consideration in the college admission process.

Should race and ethnic background be a factor in our decision making? If the invisible hand could be relied upon to produce admissions pools or employment pools that reflect the ideal of equal opportunity at all levels of society, including in the leadership positions for which Stanford prepares, special outreach would not be necessary. If the members of society mostly ignored race and ethnicity, we could forgo taking them into consideration. We hope that one day we will be able to do so.

Alas, I think it would be naïve to assume that racial and gender stereotypes do not work against many who would otherwise be capable of taking advantage of opportunities at all stages of life. In *Fires in the Mirror,* the dramatization of the Crown Heights riots of 1991 by our Stanford colleague Anna Deavere Smith, George Wolfe talks about venturing outside the African-American neighborhood in which he had grown up. I quote:

> And then I would go beyond a certain point
> I was treated like I was insignificant.
> Nobody was hosing me down or calling me nigger.
> It was just that I was insignificant.

I strongly believe it remains necessary to level the field, to recognize that there are vast differences between primary and secondary schools and how they develop ability, and to make conscious efforts to increase the presence of underrepresented minorities at all levels of society. This may even work to the advantage of a minority applicant who himself does not come from a disadvantaged economic or cultural background. It is the responsibility of educational institutions such as Stanford to find and educate those who can become the leaders of the future in a multiethnic and multiracial society. Alas, our society is quite color-conscious, and we therefore cannot yet afford to be color-blind.

I am, of course, fully aware of the fact that my view of the matter leads me to take into consideration criteria that are very problematic. There is, first of all, the utter arbitrariness of racial and ethnic labeling. Boxes to be checked may look neat on paper, but there is little underlying or inherent sense. What is race? What is *a* race? What is ethnicity? How do we deal with racial or ethnic mixing? Why is the child of a black parent and a white parent classified as black? Why does one-fourth American Indian ancestry qualify a person as Indian, while slightly less does not? Are the classificatory laws of apartheid South Africa what we end up emulating? Is our way out, self-classification, something to be fairly relied on? When government and courts dictate race relations, we quickly get caught in contradictions and absurdities.

These reservations, however, do not diminish my belief that institutions such as Stanford, if indeed they want to be universities of the highest degree, need the discretion to do as best they can in their efforts to find and educate the leaders of tomorrow. As we pursue our goals, there is no room for categorical preferences, there is no room for quotas, there is no room for preferring the unqualified over the qualified. However, there is also no room with respect to any applicant for making quantitative, scalable admissions criteria the sole touchstones of intellectual vitality, talent, character, and promise. That has never been the case at Stanford, and I hope it never will be. It is Stanford's very characteristic that it has never been one-dimensional and yet it has been able, especially over the past four decades, to become one of the world's most selective institutions. Our capacity to pursue many excellences will remain undiminished as long as we continue to get the balance right and do not waver in our commitment to quality.

I said at the outset that many who worry about the consideration of race and ethnic background in admissions and employment decisions worry about enhancing the balkanization of American society. They worry, not without justification, about institutions falling victim to highly politicized, ethnically or racially oriented groups that pursue their own narrow agendas without care for, or in direct opposition to, the overall welfare of the institution or society. Indeed, we must at all times guard against enhancing and freezing, rather than ameliorating, cleavages. We must call attention to the citizenship held in common.

The university is an institution dedicated to the search to know—the search to know of each member in her or his individual capacity. A university needs to be integrated in order to pursue its tasks. Even with affirmative action, students are evaluated and admitted to Stanford as individuals, not in groups. No university can thrive unless each member is accepted without regard to labels and stereotypes. This is the case with students, faculty, and staff. In a university, the first question in response to an argument must never be "Does he or she belong to the right group?" Instead, the only criterion must be "Is the argument valid?" An argument must never be dismissed or accepted, ignored or respected, because the speaker is male or female, black or white, American or foreign.

As concerns affirmative action policies—which raise issues that are among the most difficult that a society can confront—I think it is of the greatest importance that all those who participate in the debate refrain from demonizing their opponents.

Maintaining and furthering Stanford University is an incredibly delicate task. It is a joint intellectual and moral effort of faculty, students, trustees, alumni, and local, national, and worldwide friends. I cannot be sure about the answers to my own questions. All of us, on all sides of the issue, are and will be open to criticism. The request I have to make of those who would be critical is that they also make the effort to understand.

Context

On July 20, 1995, the Board of Regents of the University of California, at the urging of Governor Pete Wilson and regent Ward Connerly, passed resolutions prohibiting the use of race, religion, sex, color, ethnicity, or national origin as criteria for admissions, employment, and contracting at the university. In the mid-1990s, affirmative action had become an important subject in Californian politics. By the time the regents voted, a campaign, steered by Ward Connerly, to end affirmative action in state government was already well under way.

I had four major objectives when, in the summer of 1995, I sat down to draft a statement on affirmative action: (1) I wanted to make the case for affirmative action at Stanford; (2) I wanted to draw a line between Stanford as a private institution and state government and public universities; (3) I wanted to stress civility in the affirmative action discourse; (4) I wanted to approach the subject with as much candor as possible.

Before the University of California Board of Regents voted to prohibit affirmative action, Governor Wilson, who was then running for president of the United States, had issued an executive order "to end preferential treatment and to promote individual opportunity based on merit." Wilson had requested the university to take all necessary action to comply. While SP-1, the regents' resolution, made reference to the governor's executive order, the California governor does not possess the constitutional authority to determine policies for the university. He serves as regent ex officio, but is only one of twenty-six.

The Board's vote on the admissions issue was 14–10 in favor of the resolution. As if to provide a limited escape hatch, the regents introduced "disadvantage" as an admissions criterion:

> Consideration shall be given to individuals who, despite having suffered disadvantage economically or in terms of their social environment (such as an abusive or otherwise dysfunctional home or a neighborhood of unwholesome or antisocial influences), have nonetheless demonstrated sufficient character and determination in overcoming obstacles to warrant confidence that the applicant can pursue a course of study to successful completion, provided that any student admitted under this section must be academically eligible for admission.

The California Civil Rights Initiative (Proposition 209) came to a vote in November 1996 and was adopted by a majority of 55 percent (with a voter turnout of 66 percent). Technically an amendment to the California constitution, it provides that the "state shall not discriminate against, or grant preferential treatment to, any individual or group on the basis of race, sex, color, ethnicity, or national origin in the operation of public employment, public education, or public contracting." After legal challenges (which continue unabated), it went into effect in November 1997. In 2011, the California Legislature attempted to bring the state universities out from under Proposition 209 by allowing a "narrowly tailored" use of race to the extent permitted by the 2003 Supreme Court decision in *Grutter v. Bollinger* (the University of Michigan Law School case). The legislation was vetoed by Governor Jerry Brown, a supporter of affirmative action, on separation of powers grounds: it is for the courts, not the legislature, to determine the limits of Proposition 209.

Proposition 209, as enacted, had no direct implications for private universities. Had the drafters and sponsors of the proposition undertaken to extend its reach to the private sector, it would probably have caused stronger opposition than it encountered on its own terms. I was nevertheless concerned about the potential long-term effects. Would social, political, legal pressures be brought to bear on Stanford to follow the regime that now applied to the University of California? I wanted to emphasize once again that Stanford is "a private institution that has, or should have, considerable freedom in pursuit of its educational goals and ideas."

The press reaction to my statement tended to look only at my "bottom line" and to ignore the reservations and caveats. While the statement was generally well received on campus, I was subjected to scathing criticism by Thomas Sowell, a senior fellow at the Hoover Institution, and an economist. Sowell is black and a prominent critic of affirmative action. In a column for the *San Jose Mercury News,* he accused me of favoring a "body count" and of inconsistency, because, while I supported affirmative action, I also stressed that each student was to be accepted as an individual, without regard to labels. "How is that for being on both sides of the issue at the same time?"

The charge that I was trying to be on both sides of the issue at the same time was not altogether unfair. While I had strongly argued that affirmative action does not mean quotas or preferment of unqualified over qualified individuals, I had called for a substantial presence of minorities on campus (in the interest of educating leaders for a diverse and complex society). Although I did emphasize that students were admitted as individuals (to guard against enhancing and freezing "groupthink"), I also said that we could not afford to be color-blind in admissions. I truly displayed ambivalence when, on the one hand, I supported affirmative action and, on the other, strongly spoke about "the utter arbitrariness of racial and ethnic labeling." It was not that I ended up on both sides of the issues (I came down squarely on one side), but that I saw the choice Stanford faced as a moral dilemma.

Subtext

There was what might be called a subtext, though references to this "subtext" were actually quite explicit. Throughout my life as a university teacher, I have had grave reservations about the emphasis on quantitative measurements of "merit" that is so characteristic of American higher education and of how the public looks at education. The year following the affirmative action statement, in 1996, I gained some national notoriety when I picked a fight with *U.S. News and World Report* over the false precision of numerical rankings of universities by news magazines.

However, my reservations about rankings pertain to all judgments about human beings that are weighted toward scalable criteria. In the statement, I made the point that the terms "merit" and "qualified" are "occasionally" used ("often" would have been more accurate) as if they were self-defining. Instead, I said, merit depends "on many qualities of an individual and on judgments about how their combination might further the tasks of a university, government agency, or any other organization." Later in the document I called it "exceedingly narrow-minded" to pursue a one-dimensional approach to choosing those to whom we give the opportunity to study. If all we considered were capacities measurable on a scale, I argued, "without taking into consideration other aspects of being 'deserving and exceptional,' we would be betraying the Founders." Toward the end, I made the point even more emphatically when I stated there was no room "with respect to any applicant for making quantitative, scalable admissions criteria the sole touchstones of intellectual vitality, talent, character, and promise."

Postscript I

Questions concerning the significance of race at the university have arisen not only with respect to students and faculty but also involving alumni.

The subject of the relationship between the university and its minority alumni has concerned Stanford since a Board of Trustees task force in 1996 that was headed by Charles Ogletree, an alumnus, then a trustee, and a prominent member of the Harvard Law School faculty. Ogletree was also serving as the national chairman of the Stanford Fund, the university's principal annual fund-raising effort. The task force found that 98 percent of minority alumni were satisfied with their undergraduate experience, but many thought they were now "essentially out of sight." In 2002, the trustees appointed a new task force, once again headed by Professor Ogletree. The mandate of the second task force included exploration of the possibility of an "alumni of color" conference in 2004. A minority alumni weekend was indeed held that year, and the program included a panel on "diversity in perspective," composed of President John Hennessy, President Emeritus Don Kennedy, and me. I decided to raise an issue that quite a few people thought was the wrong one for the occasion.

> As many of you know I am, by academic origin, a law professor. Thus, and in order to challenge all of us, let me raise a larger normative, in a way philosophical,

question about the *future* of race and ethnic relations in our country. I shall do this by focusing on the relationship between minority alumni and the university.

University alumni are usually organized by year of graduation or, as a matter of necessity, geographically, and, to some extent, according to disciplines. These categories focus on only one characteristic of an alumnus or an alumna, that he or she is a graduate of Stanford. The point is nicely captured by our alumni clubs in foreign countries. The Stanford Alumni Association of Shanghai, or of Hong Kong, is not an organization of Chinese alumni but an organization of all Stanford graduates in the city. I confess that I am slightly apprehensive about a future that might define Stanford alumni according to racial, ethnic, or color lines.

I am even apprehensive about raising the very question this morning, but I am fortified by my mantra (taken from an opinion of Justice Brennan of the United States Supreme Court) that discussion of public issues should be "uninhibited, robust, and wide-open." While I am serious, please, take what I have to say as said in good humor. There once was a country and western song that began with the line: "Calling it love does not excuse what we are doing." It is in that spirit that I offer my observations.

They are *not* about diversity. I remain as committed to it as I have been my entire life. Shortly after I went to the University of Chicago Law School in 1966, I chaired a faculty committee that designed the law school's first affirmative action policy. I have worried about and stayed with the subject ever since, and it certainly was a main concern of mine when I had the privilege of serving as our university's, as your, president.

Some of you may recall that, in 1995, when affirmative action was under intense attack, I issued a "Statement on Affirmative Action at Stanford University." It was a defense of affirmative action. It was a strong and impassioned defense. I had thought about its every word all summer.

Toward the end of a fairly lengthy document I wrote: "I am, of course, fully aware of the fact that my view of the matter leads me to take into consideration criteria that are very problematic. There is, first of all, the utter arbitrariness of racial and ethnic labeling. Boxes to be checked may look neat on paper, but there is little underlying or inherent sense. What is race? What is *a* race? What is ethnicity? How do we deal with racial or ethnic mixing? Why is the child of a black parent and a white parent classified as black? Why does one-fourth American-Indian ancestry qualify a person as Indian, while slightly less does not? . . . These reservations, however, do not diminish my belief that institutions such as Stanford, if indeed they want to be universities of the highest degree, need discretion to do as best they can in their efforts to find and educate the leaders of tomorrow."

Given my position, you understand that I was extremely pleased to see that Justice O'Connor, in the University of Michigan affirmative action cases last term, placed considerable weight on the principle of university autonomy. In addition, however, she warned that "racial classifications, however compelling their goals, are potentially so dangerous that they may be employed no more broadly than the interest demands."

Let me take her point and turn it into a question. Is there really a necessity to continue to employ racial, ethnic, color labels in our interactions with and as graduates of the university? Or does this mean that we are employing racial classifications more broadly than the interest demands? As I said, university alumni are usually organized by year of graduation or, as a matter of necessity, geographically, and, to some extent, according to disciplines. These categories guard against enhancing and freezing cleavages. Shouldn't we stress the Stanford citizenship held in common by students and alumni?

My 1995 statement on affirmative action received much attention. Almost nobody paid any attention to its concluding remarks. I said: "A university needs to be integrated in order to pursue its tasks. Even with affirmative action, students are evaluated and admitted to Stanford as individuals, not in groups. No university can thrive unless each member is accepted without regard to labels and stereotypes. . . . In a university, the first question in response to an argument must never be 'Does he or she belong to the right group?' "

Perhaps I am unduly Panglossian about the world I observe. However, these days, when I walk across the campus, when I teach my classes, the most cheering sight is how truly "mixed-up" Stanford students seem to be as they work together, walk together, play together.

I believe that a university must be integrated in order to do its work, it must be integrated to stimulate—I am quoting from Stanford's brief in the Michigan case—"critical, reflective, and complex thinking, enhancing students' problem-solving abilities (and) . . . ability to live and work together and to communicate across racial boundaries."

One argument for affirmative action and diversity in higher education is *that* integration. Does it *not* follow that our graduates should also stress what they all have in common: the university? Maintaining and furthering Stanford is an incredibly delicate task. It is a joint intellectual and moral effort of faculty, students, trustees, alumni, and local, national, and worldwide friends. I rather doubt that that effort can succeed if, to adapt Justice O'Connor, the deviation from the norm is anything more than a temporary matter as concerns the citizenship we hold in common. In the Michigan case, Justice O'Connor wrote with respect to government use of race: "We see no reason to exempt race-conscious admissions programs from the requirement that all government use of race must have a logical end point. The Law School, too, concedes that all 'race-conscious programs must have reasonable durational limits.' "

In the interest of Stanford's present and future, but also in the interest of the country's future, shouldn't graduation mark "the reasonable durational limit," as far as the university is concerned? In asking that question I am, of course, not suggesting that we should surrender our ethnic or racial identities. At my age, it seems safe to predict that my accent will stay with me until I die. Nor am I suggesting that these identities do not greatly add richness to the world of Stanford alumni in their communities or at alumni meetings on campus. However, I am worried about how much harder the task of maintaining the many excellences of Stanford, of keeping Stanford together, and of moving it forward, becomes if the alumni, in their relation to Stanford, were to self-divide.

Postscript II

While there is no federal legal obligation that affirmative action be practiced in university admissions, the executive branch requires that federal "contractors" have affirmative action plans for their employees, faculty included, and set hiring goals based on "availability pools." Congress has generally shied away from legislating in this important area. Universities, because they receive research grants ("contracts" to do research for the federal government), are subject to the executive orders that require affirmative action.

In 1998, a major dispute developed at Stanford, when the Faculty Senate Women's Caucus submitted a report that indicated "a decline in vigilance" by the Stanford administration in efforts to maintain gender equity. Part of the background for the debate was the fact that John Shoven, then the dean of the School of Sciences and Humanities, had denied tenure to Karen Sawislak, a historian.

The significance of numbers and the progress, or lack thereof, that they indicated was interpreted differently by the provost and by the women's caucus. What few people seemed to understand was the fact that, regardless of legal requirements, the incentives to do right in terms of diversity were and are overwhelming—which is not to suggest that prejudices and set ways of doing business do not constitute real impediments.

What was also ignored in the attacks on "the" administration was that, in a university, appointments are originated not by presidents, provosts, or deans but by departments with their own sense of their needs and priorities. Furthermore, one of the greatest impediments to recruiting more women and minority faculty members is the low turnover rate of faculty, not helped any by Congress's decision to abolish mandatory retirement.

Some critics demanded a "five-year plan." Provost Condoleezza Rice and I thought such a scheme extremely ill advised. However, much of the dispute focused on the provost's strongly articulated position that affirmative action should play no role at tenure time. Regulations of the U.S. Department of Labor's Office of Federal Contract Compliance Programs (OFCCP) were invoked, statistics were argued, and—perhaps most important—Stanford history came into play through conflicting accounts of what had been the policy of Norman Wessells, dean of the School of Humanities and Sciences from 1981 to 1988.

The critics invoked a 1983 letter from Dean Wessells to then Provost Albert Hastorf in which Wessells informed Hastorf that he had turned down [*sic!*] a grievance from a woman faculty member concerning denial of tenure by the School of Humanities and Sciences. In his letter, Wessells wrote: "Stanford's Affirmative Action policy does not call for promotion of women or minority groups on the basis of lower standards than those applied to all other candidates. Rather, it requires that an especially careful scrutiny be given to assure that no consideration in the candidate's favor could be overlooked, and that in those cases that are truly borderline, where the decision could as easily go either way, the equipoise be resolved in the candidate's favor."

Whatever its meaning, the significance of this formulation of Stanford policy (in a letter confirming a denial of tenure) was questionable in view of the fact that, two years later, Wessells published a lengthy statement on "Procedures and Criteria for Appointment, Reappointment, and Promotion of Faculty in the School of Humanities and Sciences at Stanford." Wessells had taken much time to develop the paper. It had, as Wessells said in an accompanying memorandum to the faculty, the blessing of Provost James Rosse and the Advisory Board, the elected faculty body that, at Stanford, is the penultimate voice on appointments before cases reach the president.

Wessells's policy document included a special section on affirmative action that began with the sentence: "Affirmative action, an important University and School policy, is focused primarily during the time of search and appointment." The next paragraph opened with a categorical denial: "Affirmative action does not include separate standards of evaluation at the time of review for tenure or of appointment to tenure from the outside. However, in cases where a woman or a minority group candidate has qualifications equal to those of other candidates for a position, then the position should go to the affirmative action candidate." The last sentence would seem to pertain to the recruitment of tenured faculty from the outside since, at Stanford, in internal promotion cases there are never two candidates vying for the same place.

My own position, based on many years of participating in the appointments and promotion process, was that in tenure decisions (involving a lifetime commitment on the part of the university), as a matter of principle, there could be no benefit of the doubt and that past achievements had to promise future achievements. I was, of course, thoroughly aware of the role judgment played in promotion decisions, that there would often be ambiguities, and that, whatever the standard, the judgment involved human beings on all sides. To my mind, this made a clear standard even more important.

In 1999, the OFCCP began an investigation of Stanford, based on a complaint initially by fifteen women academics, alleging widespread gender discrimination and violation of affirmative action law. The investigation was apparently also prompted by some of the statements that Provost Rice had made in the Faculty Senate. The university learned of the matter through an article in the *San Jose Mercury News*.

Officially, I was informed, two weeks after the news article, of a "compliance evaluation" in a letter that began: "Your establishment located at Stanford University, Building Ten, in Stanford, California, has been selected for a compliance evaluation under Executive Order 11246, as amended." The letter also referred to my "establishment" as "your firm." At the end of February, I was also notified that OFCCP had received a class action complaint filed under Executive Order 11246, alleging various forms of discrimination against women and minority academics. It took a year for the Department of Labor to provide us with a redacted version of the complaint, though, under OFCCP's own procedures, we were entitled to an unredacted copy.

The investigation lasted more than eight years. Of the original complainants, eventually the majority dropped out for personal reasons or because the university had reached some kind of settlement with them. The Department of Labor found no discrimination or retaliation in the remaining cases. For the university and for me it was clear that there had been no systemic bias. Certainly, the provost and I had not lessened our commitment to faculty diversity. Given the many decision makers at a university, it is always possible that some faculty receive less "opportunity" than others or that violations are perceived even if none have occurred. Under these circumstances, I continue to be dismayed that certain Department of Labor spokespersons were willing publicly to single out Condi Rice as a target before any examination of the facts had taken place.

Back at the beginning of 1999, it was important to me for the Faculty Senate to understand that I agreed with the provost on tenure decisions, even if I might have stated the university's position somewhat differently or explained it more fully. On February 4, 1999, I made the following remarks in the Faculty Senate.

News reports this week juxtaposed multiple items relating to affirmative action. Across the Bay, students are suing the University of California because it allegedly *does not* practice affirmative action. Elsewhere in the country, a group is taking out ads encouraging students to sue their universities if they *do* practice affirmative action in ways to which the group objects. And closest to home, we learned from the newspapers that the Department of Labor is looking into our tenure practices.

I say "*we* learned" because I learned of the last matter in the same way as you did, by reading it in the paper. It says something about the state of our nation that even government agencies increasingly speak to the press first and to those with whom they are dealing later. After we called the appropriate Department of Labor office to inquire, we got a voicemail back yesterday saying that the office had received, quote, "some allegations," unquote, but that it had not notified us because it first must clarify the items, including whether they are covered by federal requirements. The official said, and I again quote, "It's in a very preliminary stage."

That provides a somewhat different perspective from that offered by the newspapers, one of which headlined its story, "Feds grill Stanford." I commend the *Stanford Daily* for being generally less breathless, and more accurate and intelligent, in its headline and story than most of its commercial competitors.

Perhaps more troublesome than the absence of notification or overwrought newspaper headlines, however, is a sentence in the first story to appear: "The provocative statements of Stanford's provost partly prompted the federal scrutiny, officials said." The statements referenced were about Stanford's faculty hiring and promotion philosophy, and the provost made virtually all of them here in the Faculty Senate. So it has come to this: We must be on notice that free and robust discussion of university policy in the Senate may prompt federal inquiry. If it were not sad, rather than funny, one might wonder if administrators, before attempting to answer questions from the Senate floor clearly and honestly, should be given a Miranda warning.

What many of the media stories lost sight of was that the provost was not stating a radically new theory about the role of affirmative action in faculty appointments and granting of tenure. First, her stated reservations about goals and timetables were initially expressed in response to a suggestion from the Senate floor that we publicly commit ourselves to achieving firm numerical goals on a specific timetable. I share the provost's reservations about such an idea, which could easily be seen as a quota and which has proven to be counterproductive at other universities.

Further, the provost has convincingly demonstrated that in 1985, Norman Wessells, then dean of the School of Humanities and Sciences, authoritatively established the principles she stated. I quote Dean Wessells's policy paper from fourteen years ago: "Affirmative action does not include separate standards of evaluation at the time of review for tenure."

It is long-standing Stanford policy that at the point of hiring assistant professors we practice affirmative action in casting a wide net and taking extra care to ensure that women and minorities have an equal opportunity. But at the point of tenure decision, the candidate faces evaluation entirely as an individual; at Stanford, she or he is not competing against any other candidate for the tenured position, and there is no room for anything but a judgment of the individual's merit. As one person has put it, it is just like giving grades in the classroom: In close cases, we do not give an A to members of one group and a B to members of another. Separate standards for men and women faculty members, or for any two groups, would be discrimination and contrary to the principles of equal protection and equal opportunity.

Let me clear up another misconception. To read the newspapers, one would think that women have fared badly in tenure decisions in recent years. Yet statistics that the provost presented to the Senate last May showed almost no difference between men and women. In the cohort of assistant professors hired at Stanford from 1987 through 1991—faculty members who, thus, would have come up for promotion to tenure in the last five years—50 percent of the men and 51 percent of the women were awarded tenure. Let me repeat, 50 percent of the men and 51 percent of the women.

That statistic, of course, carries the reality that half of all assistant professors hired do not gain tenure. That fact of life inevitably leaves those candidates disappointed and unhappy. But Stanford's faculty is so good precisely because, as I have previously stated, the university has no presumption that qualitatively close cases be decided in favor of the candidate for promotion. Quite the contrary, there should be no "benefit of the doubt." Appointments and promotions should be made only to the degree that past achievements promise outstanding future achievements.

As Dean Wessells made clear in 1985, it has not been Stanford's policy to promote less-qualified persons to tenure because of their race or gender. We can be assured that if we were to adopt such a policy today, we would be besieged with lawsuits by individuals who were not given such a preference. The delicate task that we face is how to satisfy the competing legal mandates that the government has set up for us if we endeavor to use other, nonpreferential, means of assuring equal opportunity. The laws Congress has passed, the regulations the executive branch has issued, and the rulings the courts have made are often hard to reconcile with one another, let alone with various state laws and regulations. Stanford, like all institutions, has learned that it is not easy to know precisely what the law dictates in the uncertain and evolving area of affirmative action, a term that is itself uncertain and evolving. An example from federal law may illustrate the difficulty of this task.

The United States Department of Labor and the California courts recently pronounced that setting flexible goals and timetables for hiring racial minorities and women is not unlawful, so long as the goals and timetables are not binding, and so long as they reflect the actual availability of qualified men and women in that particular job category. Okay, that is one position. But the United States Court of Appeals for the District of Columbia Circuit, in many ways the second-highest court in the land, held just the opposite, saying, in effect, "that is not the rule." In a unanimous opinion last year, that Court held that even such a nonbinding goal, and I quote, "pressures [employers] to maintain a workforce that mirrors the racial breakdown of their [area]," unquote, and therefore is unconstitutional [*Lutheran Church–Missouri Synod v. Federal Communications Commission*, 1998 U.S. App. LEXIS 7387 (D.C. Cir. 1998)]. There is a clear implication that such a rule would also violate the Civil Rights Act. We are left, therefore, to operate within these seemingly inconsistent legal statements.

Under Vice Provost Weisberg, we take vigorous affirmative action steps at the time of hiring, including: insisting that departments and schools follow procedures for an affirmative action search; providing statistics on the availability of women and minorities in the Ph.D. pool in the discipline in question; requiring advertising and solicitation of applications as broadly as possible; requiring documentation and justification at each level of cuts as to the effect on women and minority candidates; and providing the Faculty Incentive Fund to make certain that women and minority candidates that departments seek are not lost due to insufficient funding or overly restrictive slotting.

We examine how we are doing and we constantly strive to do better. We do our best to comply with civil rights law as we understand it and in a manner that is true to our principles.

8.

The Advantage of the Research-Intensive University

***

Peking University, Beijing

MAY 3, 1998

Text

The hundredth anniversary of China's 1898 Reforms and of Peking University [Beida] is a special occasion. It merits the gathering of university presidents from around the world. The establishment of this university signaled China's commitment to create a university that would serve the nation and the world and that would meet international standards of scholarly excellence.

The many accomplishments of Beida in the intervening years—as well as its moments of despair—are known throughout the world. At the dawn of a new century, the original vision enunciated by its early leaders is at last within grasp. Of this I am confident: All will benefit as Beida draws upon the remarkable talents of this nation to become a leading center of creativity and innovation in the twenty-first century.

But, like my university and like universities around the world, Beida faces a major question: What qualities are necessary to serve

168

society through excellence? This is the topic of my address. I am often asked to explain the "secret" ingredients of Stanford's relations with Silicon Valley. Silicon Valley has become a metaphor the world over for a productive relationship between a university and the surrounding region. And many visitors to Stanford seek to know the reasons for its success.

The answer is to be found not in some secret that Stanford has discovered but rather in its rigorous adherence to several fundamental but universal purposes and characteristics of a research-intensive university.

In using the term "research-intensive university," I mean something very specific. Systems of higher education have become highly diversified and meet a variety of needs, especially societal needs for a skilled workforce. The institutions that have emerged to face these challenges are frequently labeled "universities." There is nothing wrong with this other than definitional confusion. What I have in mind, however, is an institution that meets three criteria: it selects its students; it is primarily dedicated to the search for knowledge; and it is marked by a spirit of critical inquiry. For simplicity's sake, I shall call this the research-intensive university. I do not use the common American designation "research university" because, as will become apparent, I think of the university not as a research institute but as an institution where the intensity of research is part and parcel of the traditional university functions of teaching and learning.

What research-intensive universities need to do now, as the twenty-first century approaches, is to think much harder about what distinguishes them as institutions from other societal institutions engaged in teaching, in order to bring into sharper focus for themselves and for society what is their unique and lasting task. And while some of that thinking bears on the nonsecret I shall discuss today, its more crucial purpose is to clarify for the next century a role that was delineated most clearly nearly two hundred years ago.

To begin, I should like to go back to the last decade of the nineteenth century, the era in which both Peking University and

Stanford were founded. In the United States alone, three major universities were formed at about the same time: Johns Hopkins, Stanford, and the University of Chicago. As we know, Peking University resulted from the Hundred Day Reform of 1898 and was made the pinnacle of a multilayered educational system that was meant to modernize the education and training of officials.

An American university president who visited Beijing in 1910 observed critically that, at that time, the university was "not a well-ordered plan inspired by a lofty purpose, nor a high purpose supported by a well-ordered plan. It is rather a process, a becoming, a becoming of some sort, though of what sort it is hard to say."

It is, of course, true for all universities that they are always a "becoming," or, as I am fond of saying, that all days at a university must be "first" days. In the case of Peking University, it became clear in 1917 where the process was leading. It is at this point that similarities emerge between Peking University and Stanford University. The appointment of Cai Yuanpei as chancellor of Peking made him the real founder of a true university, one that rapidly became the foremost intellectual center of the country. Deeply influenced by his two stays in France and Germany (in Berlin and Leipzig) that amounted to a total of almost ten years, Chancellor Cai sought a synthesis of European and Chinese elements in higher education.

Cai's emphasis on university autonomy and academic freedom reflected the direct influence of the German model. The same model deeply affected the founding of Stanford, as well as Johns Hopkins and Chicago. David Starr Jordan, Stanford's first president, was an ichthyologist who read German fluently and who had been inspired by the spirit of scientific inquiry as exemplified by his role model Louis Agassiz. Agassiz in turn, was a protégé of Alexander von Humboldt. Statues of Alexander von Humboldt and Louis Agassiz still stand on the facade of Stanford's Main Quadrangle. In yet another linkage, Alexander was the famous brother of Wilhelm von Humboldt, who took on the task of rethinking Prussian universities at the beginning of the nineteenth century and developed what has become known as the Humboldtian model.

Cai and Jordan not only shared the same intellectual heritage in their thinking about universities and their commitment to the value of rational analysis and the efficacy of the scientific method but, as unlikely as it sounds, they also had somewhat similar attitudes toward the academic tasks of the individual. As Eugene Lubot has written, Cai was "by temperament and education a moralist. He often stressed the impact that neo-Confucian values, such as self-examination and self-cultivation, had upon his life."

Similarly, values of self-examination and self-cultivation were stressed continuously by David Starr Jordan. He saw them as among the main purposes of higher education, though, in his case, they obviously were derived not from Confucianism but from somewhat secularized Protestantism, with its emphasis on the autonomy of the individual.

I am stressing these shared origins because the story of Stanford (and therefore ultimately that of the relationship between Stanford and Silicon Valley) is not a story of a university that set out to become a locomotive of economic change in its region and country. Rather, it is the story of a university that, especially in the period following World War II, built on and increased its commitment to the highest-quality teaching and research, and the pursuit of innovation.

The first element of the nonsecret regarding Stanford's productive relationship with Silicon Valley is the university's fundamental commitment to the building of scholarly "steeples of excellence" in research, learning, and teaching, not to the training, as such, of engineers and business managers.

This commitment can be traced all the way to the background shared by Peking University and Stanford—Wilhelm von Humboldt and the German universities of the nineteenth century. In 1810, Humboldt wrote a memorandum entitled "On the Spirit and Organizational Framework of Intellectual Institutions in Berlin" that led to the founding of the University of Berlin. It was only ten pages in length, and constitutes perhaps the most concise reflections ever written on the university as an institution. These reflections have in no way lost their relevance, despite changes in the notion of scholarship and in the problems universities have experienced over the past two centuries.

Quite to the contrary, with universities seemingly hopelessly confused about their mission as they enter the twenty-first century, it is a matter of urgency to reflect on the university's core tasks and not be diverted by those who want the university to be all things to all people. I hope you will permit me to quote Humboldt on these matters as we continue.

The second element of Stanford's nonsecret is that in spite of innumerable temptations, it has remained an institution that sees the combination of teaching and research as what it is primarily about. Therein lies the university's advantage. In remaining true to the Humboldtian concepts shared with Peking University in its founding era, Stanford developed an enduring institutional character that at its core does not change.

Humboldt clearly recognized the dialectical nature of the relationship between research and teaching. He expressed this relationship in the following blunt formulation: The university instructor does not exist for the sake of the students.

> Both teacher and student have their justification in the common pursuit of knowledge. The teacher's performance depends on the students' presence and interest— without this, science and scholarship could not grow. If the students who are to form [the teacher's] audience did not [gather round] of their own free will, he [or she] would have to seek them out in [the] quest for knowledge. The goals of science and scholarship are worked towards most effectively through the synthesis of the teacher's and the students' dispositions. The teacher's

mind is more mature but it is also somewhat one-sided in its development and more dispassionate; the student's mind is less able and less committed but it is nonetheless open and responsive to every possibility.

Although Humboldt did much to strengthen the institution-alization of research and teaching in the university and to link the two as essential aspects of a university, the link between the two realms, in many universities around the world, has not been attained. In others, the two have become separated through the drastic reduction in funding and the relocation of research to institutions other than universities (as was the case in the former Soviet Union). The link is also nullified when teaching at the university is carried out primarily by those who have no direct relationship to research.

Not only do students profit when taught by scholars who are themselves engaged in creative endeavors; rather, scholarship itself is enriched when the younger generation consciously, if naïvely, questions it. This assumes, of course, discussion and the willingness for discussion in lectures, seminars, and laboratories.

It seems to me that in those universities overwhelmed by the sheer number of students or by hierarchical structures, or in countries in which research and teaching are fundamentally or even partially separated, much creative force lies fallow. My Humboldtian view of the matter is more radical than it may sound. My point is not what goes without saying—university teaching should be based on university research—but that university research benefits from teaching, not just from teaching graduate students but also from teaching first-year students.

The most successful method of knowledge and technology transfer on the part of the universities lies in educating first-rate students who themselves have been engaged in the search to know— men and women who will then be in a position to take on leadership roles in industry and business. Students who receive their training in university-based research arguably have a greater influence on the economy than the patentable inventions of university scientists. Therefore, attracting gifted students and interacting with them in a nonhierarchical manner is a crucial condition of success.

In this regard, I would like to cite the former dean of Stanford's School of Engineering. According to Professor James Gibbons, what students learn by participating in research during the course of their education at universities is nothing less than "the ability to think using primary principles and, in so doing, to produce innovative results."

It is precisely through the intensive participation in university research that graduate students develop the openness and curiosity that will later enable them to transfer the latest knowledge into innovative products. Outstandingly educated students are still the most meaningful contribution that university-level research has to make to technology transfer, a topic I will return to shortly.

In this context, the third important aspect of Stanford's nonsecret must be taken into consideration: the university's freedom to set agendas. Academic freedom is the sine qua non of the university. As Humboldt so nicely puts it: "One unique feature of higher intellectual institutions is that they conceive of science and scholarship as dealing with ultimately inexhaustible tasks: this means that they are engaged in an unceasing process of inquiry." Concerning government, he writes: "The state must understand that intellectual work will go on infinitely better without it." This statement, however, explicitly does not pertain to finances.

Academic freedom means, above all, freedom from politics. Insofar as this means freedom from politicians, the situation in many parts of the world nowadays is, by and large, better than in the nineteenth century. To be sure, the state and its bureaucracy anywhere frequently suffocate initiative and refuse to let in any fresh air.

Academic freedom also means freedom from pressures to conform within the university. Even Humboldt emphasized: "Intellectual freedom can be threatened not only by the government, but also by the intellectual institutions themselves, which adopt a particular point of view at their inception and then eagerly suffocate the rise of another."

It would, however, be completely out of place if academic freedom were to be interpreted as though no one has the right or responsibility to hold professors accountable for shortcomings in their teaching. This is the responsibility of the university itself. Universities must continually be occupied with the improvement of their own quality. It is hard work, often unpleasant, and, since it concerns human endeavors, perfection will never be attained. But we must begin with the notion of perfectibility. Too many of the world's universities seem to have given up the idea of working toward perfection.

In this respect, universities and politicians must worry about the imbalance that exists worldwide between the capacity of research-intensive universities and the number of students. Quality and size have a complex relationship. To be sure, it is becoming more and more urgent to make the notion of education as a form of self-learning, as a form of understanding, accessible to large numbers of people. Being able to continue to learn is more important for a man or woman of action than is the accumulation of facts for future reference. The only problem is that universities are not always the most efficient institutions for accomplishing all of this.

In the end, society suffers because, in overcrowded research-intensive universities, investments in what economists call human capital can hardly be described as optimal. The burden of numbers frequently weakens the capacity of the university to encourage the talented ones and thus stands in the way of demanding the best from them.

At the same time, the university neglects the training of those who are less gifted because it is not at all prepared for this training, or does not want to prepare itself. A culture of excellence cannot grow if a university's capacity is overtaxed.

Humboldt also insisted that the university demands a measure of solitude. Edward Shils, the great sociologist of higher education, defined the solitude postulated by Humboldt as "freedom from distraction." In the contemporary world professors, students, and the university itself are constantly being distracted, letting themselves be distracted and even seeking distraction. The temptations are endless. . . .

Among the sources for "distraction" is the area of technology transfer. Globally there exists a demand for a stronger connection and a greater partnership between universities and industry. As I said at the outset, Stanford University and Silicon Valley are seen as models for such partnerships. It is no longer a matter of debate, for instance, that northern California owes much to the presence of its universities, including of course the great University of California, and their willingness to work with industry. For example, in the 1950s, contact between Stanford University and business was made easier by the founding of the Stanford Research Park adjacent to the university. We work actively toward securing patents and licensing rights. High-tech companies in Silicon Valley alone recorded earnings of $85 billion in 1995, and according to one estimate, 62 percent of those earnings can be traced back to companies whose founders had connections to Stanford. They have created hundreds of thousands of jobs. And I am not even referring to businesses elsewhere in the United States or the world to which graduates of Stanford and other research-intensive universities have contributed.

With divisions such as Stanford's Center for Integrated Systems, we have created partnerships expressly between university and industry. However, partnerships of this sort demand relatively large investments in terms of both capital and time. The Center for Integrated Systems, which belongs to the university and possesses its own complex of buildings on campus, has as its task the integration of hardware and software systems. Represented in it are forty professors, two hundred students (largely doctoral candidates), approximately ten academic fields, and some fifteen companies from the electronics industry worldwide. The research priorities of the Center develop from meetings between researchers from the university and from industry: researchers from industry gain insights through time spent at the Center, and in turn, doctoral candidates complete internships at the companies.

This kind of partnership is not a "distraction" but an enrichment, since universities learn from their partners in industry—and therefore it constitutes the fourth essential element of Stanford's nonsecret. Such contacts strengthen the entrepreneurial spirit and the insight that technology transfer is a "bodily contact sport," that is to say, it assumes the willingness for personal interaction. This nonhierarchical interaction is very much part of the Stanford culture.

In a stimulating assessment, Annalee Saxenian, a professor at the University of California at Berkeley, has generalized this point for Silicon Valley as a whole. I quote:

> Silicon Valley has a regional network-based industrial system that promotes collective learning and flexible adjustments among specialist producers of a complex of related technologies. The region's dense social networks and open labor markets encourage experimentation and entrepreneurship. Companies compete intensely while at the same time learning from one another about changing markets and technologies through informal communication and collaborative practices; and loosely linked team structures encourage horizontal communication among firm divisions and with outside suppliers and customers. The functional boundaries within firms are porous in a network system, as are the boundaries between firms and local institutions such as trade associations and universities.

Nevertheless, one must beware of simplistic expectations. While boundaries to the business world should be porous, the research-intensive university's advantage in contributing to innovation lies in its ability to set agendas and remain open to chance and serendipity in research.

Stanford seeks continuously to maintain this openness, and the results, I believe, indicate that this aspect of its character is indeed the fifth element of the university's nonsecret. If a research-intensive university becomes dependent on the imperatives of business product development or governmental industrial policy, it loses the advantage that it gains from its commitment to the endless process of inquiry, the search to know. We also have to keep in mind that support from industry can be of great significance, but in light of the expenses involved, will not supplant research funding from the state. Basic research is a public good that business, given its orientation toward profit, can produce only in a limited quantity on its own. This is an insight governments tend to forget all too frequently, especially in times of fiscal crisis. Stanford would not be where it is today but for government funding in the period since World War II.

At the beginning of the twenty-first century, the research-intensive university, in order to make contributions to the welfare of society, must still attempt to approximate the ideal type as defined at the beginning of the nineteenth century. However, the university as an institution will be deeply influenced by information technology, which will redefine the university and its relationship to society beyond the imagination of Humboldt and the founders of both Stanford and Peking University.

Information technology is advancing so rapidly that I cannot possibly cite mastery in this area as one of Stanford's nonsecrets; however, I can say that our ability to deal with issues it raises successfully will be as critical to the university's future as any of the previous five elements of the nonsecret I have described today has been to our progress thus far.

I will focus on four areas specifically. First, there is the World Wide Web as an encyclopedic source of information, as a library, and as an archive. Today, databanks with scientific, demographic, economic, and political information are accessible worldwide, as are legal decisions, not to mention newspapers. Catalogs of the library holdings of many universities are available to researchers without the necessity of undertaking a physical trip to that library. Increasingly, the complete texts of world literature are available online, as are scholarly journals and preprints. Entire archives are being created worldwide: Government documents can be found in their entirety, photos can be reproduced, film and audio material can be downloaded. Because these databases can be searched with great specificity, and because links to relevant sites and documents are easily accessed, there are possibilities for research that, not long ago, could only be dreamed of. The web is wonderfully unlimited, robust, and open.

From the perspective of the university, what matters is that as a source of information, as a library and archive, the World Wide Web does not need a physical location at the university; thus the university's function as an organizer of knowledge and information will, in part, cease to exist.

Second, the domain of teaching is currently undergoing changes due to the new methods and forms of communication. In the near future, the "lecture" from the podium will be replaced by an interactive "presentation" in a virtual "theater" that may or may not take place in a lecture hall.

The third aspect is the most important, and one that simultaneously liberates and threatens the research-intensive university. As limitations of time and space fall by the wayside, much of what is currently tied to university teaching by those limitations will fall too. Online teaching is beginning to attain a reality that is anything but speculative. At Stanford, for example, we give highly advanced math instruction to gifted high school students the world over whose schools do not offer these courses.

The amount of instruction offered on the World Wide Web is continually increasing. Any student in any country, as long as he or she can pay the fee, can matriculate at universities that offer "cyberinstruction." Competition is evolving internationally into a tide that accreditation and testing monopolies will scarcely be able to stem. Given what I said earlier about the importance of the link between research and teaching, we have to be very careful before we accept this development as equivalent to the university as a physical institution.

Finally, the fourth aspect is the electronic links between scholars and students worldwide that already allow, for instance, for the immediate communication of new research hypotheses as well as their immediate falsification and refutation, or seminars conducted with participants in different locations. In this way, the walls of all universities will become more porous. I welcome this development that has begun to make possible the realization of an ancient dream: a worldwide "republic of learning," a global community of scholars.

But when all is said and done, the ultimate measure of a university remains in the contributions its research has made to human welfare. In that respect the university of the twenty-first century has to be measured by traditional yardsticks.

In 1954, the former American president Herbert Hoover, an alumnus of Stanford, eloquently evoked the character of universities and what they can do. The occasion was receipt of an honorary degree from the University of Tübingen, which dates back to 1477. Hoover said:

> It is by the free shuttle of ideas between our universities that we weave the great tapestries of knowledge. Our academic traditions have developed a system that is peculiarly effective in spotting outstanding intellects and putting them to work in a climate that fosters creative, original thinking.
>
> From the mutual building by our university faculties and laboratories devoted to abstract science have come most of the great discoveries of natural law. The application of these discoveries through invention and

production has been the task of the engineers and technicians whom we train. Applied science dries up quickly unless we maintain the sources of discovery in pure science. From these dual activities of the scientists and the technicians, a great stream of blessings in health, comfort, and good living has flowed to all our people.

Today I have attempted to stress why, for Stanford, being part of that great stream has had very little to do with secrets and a great deal to do with adherence to the fundamental purposes and character of a research-intensive university. A commitment to building "steeples of excellence" in research, learning, and teaching; viewing the combination of teaching and research as what we are about, despite innumerable temptations; having the freedom to set agendas; seeking industry partnerships as enrichments to, not distractions from, the research process; maintaining porous boundaries; and being open to chance and serendipity in research—these are the nonsecrets.

Their source is the common wellspring from which Stanford and Peking University both were drawn and from which blessings will continue to flow for our nations, and for all mankind, in the twenty-first century.

Context

Peking University is the English language name for Beijing Daxue (nicknamed Beida). In the 1970s, after the People's Republic of China decided to adopt the pinyin system for the Romanization of Chinese words, the university, for a short while, was known as Beijing University. In order to avoid confusion with other universities in Beijing, the Peking designation was resumed in 1980. The letters PKU serve as a short reference. At the time of its founding in 1898, PKU was called Imperial University of Peking.

For the centennial celebration in 1998, postal authorities issued commemorative stamps that were provided to the centenary participants. The accompanying text read: "Drawing on thousands of years of heritage, a great school has thrived for a hundred years. The centennial celebrations of the founding of Peking University, China's first national comprehensive university, are a grand occasion for Chinese education, drawing it more than ever into the international spotlight." The statement that the school drew "on thousands of years of heritage" was perhaps an indication of the rediscovery of Confucianism that has grown ever stronger in recent decades. However, an article in the *China Daily* at the time of the centennial referred to Beida as "the cradle of the country's avant-garde ideas, including Marxism, democracy, science, free marriage and the shareholding system."

China has more than two thousand colleges and universities. In internal Chinese rankings of universities, Peking University, Tsinghua, Fudan, Nanjing, the Chinese University of Science and Technology, and Shanghai Jia Tong University congregate at the top, with the competition between the two major Beijing institutions, PKU and Tsinghua, perhaps the most intense. In international rankings, especially those conducted by Shanghai Jia Tong University, where Harvard and Stanford lead worldwide, PKU and Tsinghua do not rank anywhere near the top.

The centenary of PKU provided the Chinese leadership once again with an opportunity to stress the crucial role of science and education in development and to emphasize the need for openness to scientific achievements elsewhere in the world. Ever since Deng Xiaoping's speech at the 1978 National Science Conference in which he stressed the need for "high speed development of science and technology," Chinese universities have emerged from the nightmares of the Cultural Revolution. More than twenty years after its end and almost ten years after Tiananmen Square, the leading Chinese universities were eager to innovate and establish contacts around the world.

The main event of PKU's centennial was a celebration on May 5, 1998, in the Great Hall of the People at which Jiang Zemin, Deng Xiaoping's successor as the PRC's leader, spoke. At the event, attended by about eight thousand people (including some eighty university presidents, vice chancellors, and rectors from all over the world), Jiang Zemin praised Peking University for its traditions of "patriotism, progress, democracy, and science"—formulaic attributes that were mentioned repeatedly in connection with Beida's centennial. He then went on to say: "The modernization of China must center on economic reform and stick to the strategy of revitalizing China through science and education." One of the means Jiang wanted employed was the establishment of world-class universities in China. Peking University and Tsinghua were singled out for additional financial support on the road to global status.

Immediately preceding the official ceremony, Peking University, under the chairmanship of Chen Jiaer, a nuclear physicist and its president, had called a two-day conference on "The University of the Twenty-First Century." The conference drew many Chinese and foreign participants and had been organized by Professor Min Weifang, a Stanford Ph.D. in education, who for many years served as executive vice president of Beida.

It was at this conference that I delivered the text that has been placed at the beginning of this chapter. Understandably, the organizers had asked me specifically to address Stanford's role in relation to its Silicon Valley environment. My views on that matter had been deeply influenced by James Gibbons, former dean of the Stanford School of Engineering and an adviser to me on university-industry relations. However, as is clear from the text, I conceived of my subject much more broadly and dealt with issues and norms that had preoccupied me on many prior occasions.

The proceedings of the forum were subsequently published by Peking University Press and received a fair amount of attention. Since the speeches had also been videotaped, it seems that they were broadcast repeatedly on China Central Television. I have the recollection that, for many months, visitors to China would return and mention to me that they had watched my talk at some hotel somewhere in China. Whether it had been censored or not, I, of course, do not know.

I used the opportunity of my visit to enter into discussions with President Chen and Professor Min about opening a Stanford overseas studies program at Beida and, during the summer of 1998, Stanford representatives began serious negotiations with their PKU counterparts and the hope was to conclude these preparations by the time Min Weifang was scheduled to visit Stanford in November of 1998.

In my speech, I had said that academic freedom was the sine qua non of the university and that academic freedom meant, above all, freedom from politics. As I delivered these remarks, I was unaware of the fact that China was holding, in a Beijing prison, a Stanford research associate from our Center for International Security and Arms Control (now the Center for International Security and Cooperation [CISAC]).

Hua Di had been arrested in Beijing on January 5, 1998, a few days after he had returned to Beijing in response to an invitation to help in the development of U.S.-China relations. Before his departure for Beijing, Hua had received in-person assurances from state security officials in Hong Kong that he would not face any legal problems. Hua, then in his early sixties, was a Chinese citizen with permanent residency status in the United States. He suffered from a rare cancer for which he was being treated at home in California.

Hua, a high-ranking Chinese missile expert, had first spent time at Stanford in the early 1980s as a visiting scholar. He was on a trip to (then still British) Hong Kong when, following the bloodletting at Tiananmen Square, he decided not to return home and instead made arrangements to come to Stanford. Hua was appointed a research associate at CISAC in 1989 and was an active participant in its Project on Peace and Cooperation in the Asian-Pacific Region. He and John Lewis, a Stanford professor of political science, cowrote articles, including a history of the Chinese ballistic missile program. After his arrest in early January 1998, Hua Di was charged with betraying state secrets.

I did not know Hua and was blindsided by faculty who had learned about his detention more or less immediately but failed to inform their university's president. Their desire was to keep the story as quiet as possible. John Lewis wrote to President Jiang as early as January 28, 1998. In his letter, Lewis took the position that the source materials for publications written by him and Hua were provided by approved Chinese authorities or already published and available in Stanford libraries. I learned about the matter in the early fall of 1998, many months after my return from the PRC, when press reports appeared in the Asian and Western press.

On September 24—I was abroad—Provost Rice wrote President Jiang asking for Hua's release on humanitarian grounds. It was our understanding that Hua's cancer had gotten worse in the absence of appropriate medical treatment. On October 30, 1998, I followed up with a public statement to the faculty senate in which I urgently repeated our request for Hua's freedom and stressed that the arrest was chilling for all those who favored academic collaboration between Western universities and the PRC. Numerous interventions followed from highly placed current and former United States government officials and prominent Stanford administrators and faculty. All of these pleas were deigned unworthy of an answer by Jiang Zemin or other Chinese authorities.

In the October faculty senate meeting, I was asked whether I planned to take "the symbolic gesture of stopping any ongoing academic conversations" between Stanford and China concerning the planned program at Peking University. According to the minutes, I replied cautiously: "The arrest and continued detention of Hua Di has clearly given rise to wariness on my part."

I, of course, did not know for certain whether the claim that Hua had violated Chinese law was baseless. The circumstances of his detention suggested political influences and arbitrariness. Given that rule of law and academic freedom remain precarious concepts in China, the treatment of Hua Di was the very opposite of a confidence-building measure.

During Min Weifang's previously scheduled visit on November 30, 1998, I informed him that Stanford, for the time being, would not proceed with plans to open a program at Beida. I did not think that it was appropriate for me to enter into an agreement with one of China's most prominent institutions—continue, as it were, as if nothing had happened—while a Stanford researcher was being held in prison without any explanation. I certainly did not take the step to suspend our discussions lightly, since throughout my life, throughout the many years of the Cold War, I had always favored engagement rather than iron curtains.

In 1999, Hua was tried in Beijing, convicted, and sentenced to fifteen years in prison. A higher court overturned the conviction because it found the evidence unclear. This was generally regarded as unprecedented and gave us hope. However, on retrial, Hua was convicted again. The second time he received a sentence of "only" ten years. Subsequent efforts to free him were to no avail.

Postscript

In 2004, Stanford's Bing Overseas Studies Program opened at Peking University. I did not oppose the step. The fact that we had been ineffective in helping Hua Di gave us every reason to remain wary but should not permanently stand in the way of the university's engagement. Peking University has remained deeply interested in bilateral ties with Stanford. In 2012, President Hennessey dedicated the Stanford Center at Peking University consisting of teaching, study, research, and conference facilities. The center is housed on campus (actually on the grounds of a former imperial palace) in the newly constructed Lee Jung Sen building, which is named for a PKU alumnus who is the father of Chien Lee, a Stanford alumnus and former member of the Board of Trustees.

Hua Di has completed his sentence and, to the satisfaction of his Stanford friends, was able to attend the dedication of the Lee Jung Sen Building on March 21, 2012. I was able to meet with Hua Di in October 2012 when in Beijing for a visit to the Stanford center.

9.

Thinking in a Free
and Open Space

Commencement Convocation, Graduate School of
Arts and Sciences, Yale University

MAY 25, 2003

Text

Thank you, Dean Salovey. As Dean Hockfield (whom I greatly admired as dean) has become Yale's provost, I am much comforted by the fact that the fate of the Graduate School of Arts and Sciences will now, like the presidency of Yale University, be in the hands of a Stanford alumnus. In case some members of the audience suspect Stanford nepotism in the choice of me as the convocation speaker, I should like to stress that I was invited by then Dean Hockfield. Dean Salovey's only involvement was that he did not withdraw the invitation when I offered him the opportunity.

As probably all the graduates in the audience know, the Connecticut "Act for Liberty to erect a Collegiate School" from 1701 that led to the founding of Yale, had for its purpose to instruct "youth" in the arts and sciences and "fit" them "for Publick employment both in Church & Civil State." While, three hundred years onward, the formulation strikes one as overly directive, not to say autocratic, it makes clear that, from its very beginnings, Yale was dedicated to public service.

And indeed, the university has always taken great pride in the fact that many of its alumni enter public service in one form or another. There will be those among you who will continue that tradition. Today, however, I do not primarily want to talk about public service in the ordinary sense of the term, but I want to use this occasion to thank you, the graduates, for the public service you have rendered to date by pursuing graduate studies. I should like to talk about the university *as* public service, not the university *and* public service.

During your college years, elsewhere or here, and during the often many (I hope not *too* many) years you have spent in Yale's Graduate School of Arts and Sciences, you have been engaged in one of the most noble and honorable forms of public service I know. That is, you have promoted the public welfare through the increase of knowledge: your own knowledge, your fellow students' knowledge, your faculty's knowledge, and society's knowledge.

I hope you found this public service frequently exhilarating. Yet I also know, from my own experience, how lonely, anomic, discouraging it can be: how conflicted one often is between one's commitment to learning, research, and teaching, on the one hand, and one's other wishes and preferences, on the other.

Hannah Arendt, the political philosopher, wrote her dissertation with the guidance of Karl Jaspers, then a professor of philosophy at Heidelberg, on the concept of love in Saint Augustine. Jaspers was somewhat critical of what he thought was insufficient scholarly objectivity and rigor on her part. She had to do a new draft, which she sent him in June 1929, accompanied by a letter from which I quote the beginning.

Dear Professor Jaspers,

Please forgive me for sending you the second, revised version of my dissertation only now, contrary to all my earlier expectations. Benno von Wiese has no doubt told you the most important reason for the delay. I was married four weeks ago. I hope you will understand why I did not let you know earlier myself, but the completion of my work weighed on me, and I did not want to write to you with personal news before I had fulfilled my scholarly obligations.

You know it all: the expectations, the delays, the conflicts between scholarly and private commitments. Arendt wrote about fulfilling her scholarly obligations. As I knew Hannah Arendt personally, I can say, with conviction, that what she meant primarily was not her undertakings to her dissertation adviser but her obligations to scholarship as such.

I congratulate you and your families and your friends, who are with you today, on your fulfilling your scholarly obligations, whether in Masters or in Ph.D. programs. I welcome you to the ancient and honorable company of scholars, and, on behalf of the worldwide republic of learning, I thank you for having chosen the path of which you mark an important stage today.

But, as Warren Harding, twenty-ninth president of the United States, once said, in what has become one of my favorite mixed metaphors, "One must not drop anchor until one is out of the woods." I now apply the advice about not dropping anchor until out of the woods to you. Indeed, I remind you with another mixed metaphor that "the future is an uncharted sea full of potholes."

A stark fact of your future lives as scientists, scholars, researchers, teachers, or in some other role, is that you will never be out of the woods—even if you have a job secured. This is both the bad and the good news. When I teach a class, I am still as nervous as I was in my first year as an assistant professor about whether I truly appreciate the complexities of my subject matter and whether I really know how to teach it—perhaps I am more nervous now than I was then.

However this may be, I should like to return to the public service aspect of universities or, more precisely, a public service that I hope you will render, having, by and large, equipped yourselves to do so through your graduate work. Let me make four simple points.

First. Do not let the future make you narrow in intellect, spirit, pursuits, values. Robert Oppenheimer, the physicist, in 1932 wrote to his younger brother, who seemed to be settling on too particular an intellectual course: "Let me urge you with every earnestness to keep an open mind: to cultivate a disinterested and catholic interest in every intellectual discipline, and in the non-academic excellences of the world, so that you may not lose that freshness of mind from which alone the life of the mind derives, and that your choice, whatever it be, of work to do, may be a real choice, and one reasonably free."

And—my second point—remember throughout life what an unidentified French theologian once said: The most corrupting lies are problems poorly stated. In research, as you experienced throughout your graduate studies, the poorly stated problem stands in the way of achieving results. In public affairs, the poorly stated problem may become a "corrupting lie," that is, a moral issue, not merely an obstacle to finding solutions.

My third point. The search to know has always been characterized by the need to doubt, the need to be critical, including the need to be self-critical. The task is to look not just for the evidence to support propositions you like, but for the counterevidence as well.

My fourth point is that I implore you to apply the reasoning habits you have developed as graduate students at Yale, especially the habit to search for the counterevidence, to the public affairs of our country (or your home country if you are not from here) and of the world. In short, continue the particular public service that you have been engaged in as graduate students when you act as citizens in the public realm. That request is not as obviously met as you may think. Throughout my life, I have been amazed by scholars who, in some matter of public concern, jumped to conclusions with a speed and lack of evidence they would never have accepted in their respective disciplines.

I should like to return to Arendt and Jaspers. In 1948, Arendt, the Jewish refugee who had fled Germany in 1933, at that time abandoning any hope for an academic career, dedicated a book of essays to her former teacher. She wrote:

> What helped me, in the years to follow, to find my way through reality without surrendering to it in the manner in which, in former times, one used to strike a bargain with the devil, is what I learned from you: only truth, not ideology, matters; one must live and think in a free and open space rather than in a shell however beautifully furnished; necessity, in any shape, is only a specter that wants to lure us into playing a particular role instead of attempting to be human, as best we understand. What I have never forgotten is the way you listened (so difficult to describe), the tolerance that was always ready to be critical—equally far removed from skepticism and fanaticism—and that, after all, only expressed the insight that all human beings partake of reason and no human being is infallible.

I myself, many years later, had an opportunity to meet Karl Jaspers in Basel, where he had moved after World War II. I experienced the way he listened, "the tolerance that was always ready to be critical," a reflective reticence that was the very opposite of living and thinking in a shell. Much of public life, on the left and on the right, and including government, seems to be conducted in ideological shells instead of by the "reasoned engagement" that Yale's president, Richard Levin, stressed a year ago in his "Thinking About September 11." I hope you will stay away from shells, however elaborately furnished.

Tomorrow, you will be awarded formal citizenship in the worldwide "republic of learning," a "free and open space" that ranges from

Yale to Tokyo, from Stanford to Chicago to Florence, and that is characterized by a common standard of *reasoned* engagement. I congratulate and welcome you as fellow citizens.

Context

Susan Hockfield, then dean of the Graduate School of Arts and Sciences at Yale, had invited me to deliver the 2003 commencement address. By the time of commencement she had become Yale's provost (later to assume the presidency of MIT), while Peter Salovey, after succeeding Hockfield as dean, became dean of the college, then provost, and in 2012 was elected to follow Richard Levin as president of Yale.

American universities place a fair amount of emphasis on public service. They have done so for a long time: Yale for more than three hundred years. In most countries, as students enter college or university, they also embark on a high degree of specialization. Put differently, higher education institutions elsewhere, generally, do not undertake a curricular responsibility to promote a fuller and better general understanding of the world on the part of *all* their students or to foster an explicit commitment to public service. Tertiary education occurs in relatively narrow and diversified channels. The American undergraduate college, on the other hand, has general education requirements (however weakly implemented), often including an "education for citizenship" component.

The founding grant of Stanford University referred to "promotion of the public welfare" as the purpose and, in 1902, Jane Stanford elaborated in a speech to the Board of Trustees

> The moving spirit of the Founders in the foundation and endowment of the Leland Stanford Junior University was love of humanity and a desire to render the greatest possible service to mankind. The University was accordingly designed for the betterment of mankind

morally, spiritually, intellectually, physically, and materially. The public at large, and not alone the comparatively few students who can attend the University, are the chief and ultimate beneficiaries of the foundation. While the instruction offered must be such as will qualify the students for personal success and direct usefulness in life, they should understand that it is offered in the hope and trust that they will become thereby of greater service to the public.

While Jane Stanford's observations sound extremely lofty, the realization of these goals was supposed to occur indirectly through "advanced instruction and original research." "The paramount purpose of the Founders of the Leland Stanford Junior University" was "to promote the public welfare *by* [emphasis added] founding, endowing, and having maintained a University with the colleges, schools, seminaries of learning, mechanical institutes, museums, galleries of art, and all other things necessary and appropriate to a University of high degree."

For Jane Stanford, service to humanity did not mean that the university should take on political roles. She was extremely wary of politics. In the same 1902 speech (it constituted a formal amendment of the Founding Grant) Stanford demanded: "The University must be forever maintained upon a strictly nonpartisan and nonsectarian basis. It must never become an instrument in the hands of any political party or any religious sect or organization."

How to reconcile academic freedom with the goal of remaining "strictly nonpartisan" is a question that has not become any easier to answer since the days when Mrs. Stanford insisted that President Jordan, in 1900, force the resignation of Edward Ross, an economist later turned sociologist, for the Populist-Progressive views he had expressed publicly (and in the classroom) about such issues as railroads, silver, and Asian immigration (he was a Nativist). Julius Weinberg, Ross's biographer, comments that he is "perhaps best remembered for his militant advocacy of melioristic sociology—a sociology dedicated to the cause of social reform." The American Association of University Professors owes its founding to the debate over *Lehrfreiheit* that was caused by Ross's dismissal.

Before and during the years I was president, there was much discussion at Stanford about how the university could encourage its students to engage in public service. The debate was cast in terms of the university *and* public service. In that discussion, participants sometimes lost sight of the fact that the university *as* public service is our primary mission.

As I quoted in the Preface, the Commission on Undergraduate Education at Stanford that I appointed in 1993 and that was chaired by Professor Sheehan said in its report: "The university should encourage many qualities of mind and spirit—a potential for leadership, a devotion to public service, an appreciation of beauty—but its special mission, and its distinctive contribution to the well-being of society, is to demonstrate the value of free inquiry and tolerant debate by engaging its students in the search for knowledge."

While I strongly favor student commitment to public service, I have been concerned about the potential for underestimating the need to start with relevant knowledge, the potential for embracing superficial notions of the public interest, the potential for underestimating the opportunity costs of public service pursuits while at the university. I used my welcome to Stanford freshmen and their parents in September of 1998 to address essentially the same topic that I again took up, in slightly different form, in 2003 at Yale while I was serving as a member of the Yale Corporation. I said: "Involvement in public service while here provides you, in your role as citizens, with a chance to make yourselves as effective as possible by applying the same critical reasoning and honest pursuit of knowledge to public service that are otherwise prized within the university."

10.

Coda

The literature on universities in modern societies is prodigious. It covers the choice and admission of students and fee levels, the choice of faculty and curricula, the choice among different approaches to teaching and teaching technologies, the choice of research agendas, the choice of governance structures, the choice of investments in programs, infrastructure and funding sources, the choice of knowledge transfer strategies, the choice of ways to bring about innovation pure and simple and innovation at the university to increase productivity, the choice among approaches to the challenges of globalization, et cetera, et cetera, et cetera. My listing makes clear that myriad choices have to be made in order to determine strategies that are appropriate for a given university.

These are the best of times and the worst of times for universities worldwide. These are the best of times, because, in even the most remote corners of the globe, it is hard to find anybody who does not willingly acknowledge the importance of universities in the knowledge-based global economy. Even countries that are rich in natural resources are looking for alternative ways to secure their economies in the long run. Government investments in innovative research and knowledge transfer—from universities to their students, to governments, and to businesses—are the talk of politicians everywhere.

These are the worst of times for universities, especially public ones, because as governments face tight budgets, they do not generally assign higher education and research funding the priority that their emphasis on the need for innovation would suggest. They neither put their money where their mouth is nor even remotely understand the amounts of money and time it takes to create "world class" universities, if that is the goal. Nor do they understand that it takes but a few years to diminish eminent institutions severely. Many of the great public universities of the United States are endangered.

"The search to know" is a good phrase to summarize what all universities are about, however narrow or broad their purposes may otherwise be. It captures why there are students (they want to learn, to know something, they want to enhance their career prospects), what faculty are engaged in as they pursue learning, develop courses, and pursue research, and what differentiates good universities from many other societal institutions.

That differentiation is crucial. The university's distinct ways in its quest for learning should not be determined by politics or the marketplace. In his inaugural address as president of the University of Chicago, Edward Levi spoke about the early days of that university: "The university's seriousness of purpose was proven from the first by its insistence upon freedom of inquiry and discussion. Intellectual tests for truth made other standards irrelevant. . . . The emphasis on the need to question and to reexamine, as part of both the inquiry of research and the inquiry of teaching, established a basic unity for all of the university." Inquiry must be carried out by critical analysis according to standards that themselves are subject to examination and reexamination.

To make "other standards irrelevant," the university also must be scrupulously cautious about entanglements. Universities have never been (nor should they be) ivory towers. But how much direct involvement with the economy or, for that matter, societal problem solving can any university afford without risking the disinterested pursuit of knowledge?

The question of what universities are for is receiving an increasingly narrowed answer that is extremely broad in its ambition.

Universities are asked to address global challenges in directed multidisciplinary efforts and to develop policies for the improvement of the economy, environment, health, democracy, governmental institutions, and so forth. The governor of California, Jerry Brown, recently called on scientists to become "missionaries" about global climate change. It is well nigh impossible to express reservations about these calls to political action without appearing callous and out of touch with the real world.

In raising the question about what is being urged on universities and about where universities are headed, I am not a romantic who believes in citadels of pure learning: I have been, after all, a student, a faculty member, a dean, a provost, a president. I am now a faculty member once again. I certainly do not believe we have any reason to look down our noses at industry and other businesses or at government. And, of course, we have every reason to take seriously student concerns about their career prospects.

However, the American system of higher education is a highly differentiated system, which has found diverse solutions to meet various expectations and needs. Within that system, we continue to need universities that emphasize, over everything else, the disinterested pursuit of knowledge in teaching, learning, and research.

What I am concerned about is the danger that, by stressing their immediate utility all universities—including the very best—are losing their distinctness. We must convince our societies that they would be poorer but for the continued investment in institutions that combine the rigorous tradition of knowledge and the rigorous search for truth with the excitement of frequently serendipitous discovery in a setting of institutional autonomy. Vannevar Bush, in "Science, the Endless Frontier," emphasized: "One of the peculiarities of basic science is the variety of paths that lead to productive advance. Many of the most important discoveries have come as a result of experiments undertaken with very different purposes in mind."

As academic researchers engage in activities and advocacies, political or business, it will become much harder for them not to "jump with their preconceptions" or to falsify their hypotheses. It will also be harder for them not to distinguish between "friends" and "enemies" among their scholarly colleagues. As universities engage in directed, policy-oriented approaches, they must even more than ever dedicate themselves to Thomas Huxley's admonition: "My business is to teach my aspirations to conform themselves to facts, not to try and make facts harmonize with my aspirations."

In addition to risking disinterestedness, entanglements risk—if indeed there is anything left to risk—what Edward Shils called "freedom from distraction." Professors, students, and the university itself are constantly being distracted, letting themselves be distracted, and even seeking distraction.

The temptations are endless as universities and their members are expected to make their expertise available to government and business worldwide, to improve the speed of innovation, to participate in the improvement of social conditions, to directly contribute to a higher quality of life. Small wonder that many universities have become unfocused and frequently believe they need to be all things to all people.

As David Kennedy, the Stanford historian, has recently said about Silicon Valley: "The entire Bay Area is enamored with these notions of innovation, creativity, entrepreneurship, mega-success. It's in the air we breathe out here. It's an atmosphere that can be toxic to the mission of the university as a place of refuge, contemplation, and investigation for its own sake."

General policies that try to create ivory or iron walls will not help in this regard. The activities into which faculty and students are tempted are often high-value activities. Furthermore, as Henry Rosovsky, the former dean of the Harvard Faculty of Arts and Sciences, has pointed out, intense competition among universities has greatly increased the power of professors and "given many of them immunity from institutional control."

To the extent to which universities still have a measure of such control, there is no other way for their leadership and faculties than to make categorical *and* case-by-case judgments about what should *not* be done in order to protect the university's distinct ways. These judgments must be based on demanding and rigorous conflict of commitment and conflict of interest analysis. It is quite possible to have rules and to enforce them. The job—to use one of George Shultz's favorite metaphors about diplomacy—is one of gardening: "Getting out the weeds when they are still small" and thinking very hard about what new trees to plant.

In his book *The New New Thing,* Michael Lewis writes that "the business of creating and foisting new technology upon others that goes on in Silicon Valley is near the core of the American experience. . . . The United States obviously occupies a strange place in the world. It is the capital of innovation, of material prosperity, of a certain kind of energy, of certain kinds of freedom, and of transience. Silicon Valley is to the United States what the United States is to the rest of the world."

As universities strive to become capitals of innovation, they must strenuously avoid becoming "capitals of transience" as well. Quite to the contrary, universities have the responsibility to remain concerned with fundamentals, including the human condition, human values, the arts, history, traditions. There are many facets of the university that should *not* change. It is the university's responsibility to take the long view of everything. Yes, we are a source of innovation; yes, we are open to change. Our commitment, however, should be to the search to know as such, to the pursuit of truth, even though we realize, with Robert Musil, that the "truth is not a crystal that can be slipped into one's pocket, but an endless current into which one falls headlong." I might add, a current that one should not leave in one's lifetime.

As universities pursue new knowledge, as they encourage their graduates to be entrepreneurial, they need also assure that our world does not get flatter and paler, that the layered quality of life remains part of our life. To quote Karol Berger's *A Theory of Art:* "We need images and representations, we need above all stories to give ourselves an identity and to give our existence a depth of significance. Without representations of history and art with which to compare our own experiences, our world would be appallingly flat, one-dimensional, and impoverished, the world deserving Henry James's bleak characterization . . . : 'what you see is not only what you get, it is all there is.' "

Beginning with my inaugural address, I have always called for reconsideration of the university's work and asked that all days at the university be thought of as *first* days for us to inquire what we can do better, but also what we must retain and maintain. One of the most perplexing questions concerning the coming "first days" is what impact communication technologies, especially online learning, will and should have on our institutional existence. As early as about twenty years ago, *Forbes* opined, in the present tense: "Colleges and universities as we know them *are* obsolete" [my emphasis].

Before we agree, it makes sense to differentiate among the various roles universities play in the world. One can distinguish at least nine tasks that universities perform: (1) knowledge assessment, tradition, and creation; (2) assessing and reviewing those who have the capacity to become and be scholars; (3) education (including professional education) and learning; (4) fostering a worldwide community of scholars; (5) knowledge transfer; (6) credentialing; (7) social integration; (8) the collegiate rite of passage to adulthood; and (9) providing a place for "networking."

When one looks at the university this way, it is hard to believe that all of these functions can and will migrate to cyberspace. Some, however, or portions of some, have already done so or will do so in the future. Given the great opportunities for technology-supported improvements in teaching and learning, there will be a significant measure of global substitution of online learning and other online interactions for in-residence education. We have no reason to be complacent.

While I am concerned about complacency, I am also concerned about more far-reaching implications of what John Hennessy has called the "coming tsunami." It is possible that commercial providers of online educational services will skim off what for them is profitable and will leave the universities with everything that is expensive in education and research. Since, as I never tire of saying, research and teaching have a dialectical relationship, it would be tragic for both if the two core aspects of the university became more separated. Therefore, we need to be articulate about that relationship, in particular at our leading research-intensive universities.

And then there are the challenges to the institutional cohesiveness that online education and the Internet pose. The more scattered academic work becomes, the less easy it will be to sustain the noncommunitarian community that is the university, the less easy it will be to sustain the institutional culture on which the freedoms of the university depend.

While the further globalization of knowledge is highly desirable, it comes at a price. If I may quote Stephen Stigler:

> It seems plausible that [the] expanding electronic network will eventually lead to a weakening of our sense of institutional identity and a fundamental change in the intellectual competition that organizes our enterprise. Individual faculty may be in closer contact with collaborating colleagues at other universities (or with graduate students working under their direction in other countries) than with faculty and students in slightly different specialties down the hall. The importance of the geographic unit may be eclipsed by intellectual disciplinary units that are international in scope. For the immediate future financial resources that are administered by geographically-constrained universities may restrict the scope of any reconfiguration, but in time even that constraint may diminish, leaving the present research universities effectively operating themselves as foundations

supporting international, highly specialized, disciplinary graduate schools.

The prospect of the university of the twenty-first century is that of a forum without clear borders. At present almost all universities continue to be national institutions. Included in this category are the very best universities in the United States—universities that, in many ways, already are international utilities, but financed overwhelmingly nationally. I confess that it is very difficult for me to imagine a global republic of learning without traditional country-based universities as major elements. However, a combination of a weakening sense of identity with a dwindling of national sources of support may eventually undermine traditional structures.

The university as a concrete institution at a specific location and as a form of organization for the pursuit of coexistent and compatible goals under special conditions will have to confront these conditions, as well as think through the conditions that underlie its work. For instance, it is far from obvious to me that universities should become "multinationals" with branches all over the globe.

The research-intensive university will survive only to the extent that it is irreplaceable. But what is it about the university that is most irreplaceable? Probably the link between teaching and research in the laboratory and the classroom, the working environment for professors and students that requires a particular brand of camaraderie that both assumes and makes possible this environment. As large-class instruction, even in the best universities, is likely to migrate online, it is the inclusion of students at all levels in research endeavors that will continue to provide unparalleled opportunities to know.

In 1791, Goethe gave a short talk on the need of artists and scholars for the company of others:

> The friends of science often find themselves . . . isolated
> and alone, although the widespread availability of books

and the rapid circulation of knowledge makes them immune to their own lack of companionship. . . . Thus we owe inestimable benefits and an unmistakable usefulness to the printing press and the freedoms it has bestowed upon us; but there is another sort of usefulness connected to the greatest feeling of satisfaction that we owe to lively interaction with educated beings and the candidness of this interaction. Often, a gesture, a word, a warning, a cheer, a contradiction is, at the right time, able to change us for the better . . .

What Goethe described as the "rapid circulation of knowledge" by means of the printing press has now become, with the help of information and communications technology, an *immediate* global circulation. This development, too, has brought with it an "unmistakable usefulness." But it will, I hope, no more replace the "lively and candid interaction with educated beings" in the university than the printing press did.

Acknowledgments

In the case of a book that is based on a long life in academia, acknowledgments have a very arbitrary character. I have benefited from many influences and much advice that is reflected in the book, but that often cannot easily be traced. The dilemma is substantial. I have therefore decided to name only those persons to whom I recall giving various texts to critique.

I had the great good fortune to have three outstanding provosts: the late Jerry Lieberman (my first year as president), Condoleezza Rice for six years, and John Hennessy for one year before he became my successor. With each of them I had an exemplary working relationship, and while they served in the provost's office, each of them reviewed critically whatever I asked them to review and gave me feedback on everything that was on my mind.

The same is true for senior Stanford executives or senior staff: Alan Acosta, Mariann Byerwalter, Jean Chu, Geoffrey Cox, John Ford, Larry Gibbs, Larry Horton, Stephen Peeps, Lowell Price, Michael Roster, Terry Shepard, Bill Stone, Tim Warner, Jacqueline Wender, and Debra Zumwalt. Geoff Cox, in particular, provided research and drafts on a variety of issues. Throughout the many years of our collaboration, Terry Shepard has been a fearless editor.

Research assistance for some parts of the speeches or other text was given by Ingrid Deiwiks, Tom Fenner, Maggie Kimball, and Gene Mazo. Ingrid Deiwiks has been my executive assistant for twenty years and is still indispensable.

The book manuscript was read in toto or in part and commented on by Bliss Carnochan, Geoffrey Cox, Patricia Graham,

John Hennessy, Michael Keller, David Kennedy, Richard and Jane Levin, John Lillie, Phil Neal, Henry Rososvsky, Michael Roster, James Sheehan, Terry Shepard, Philip Taubman, and Marilyn Yalom. All of them are friends to whom I am indebted in many ways. I am also much indebted to my editors at Yale University Press, Eric Brandt and Dan Heaton.

Sid Drell and Phil Taubman helped with the title. Sid Drell, Lucy Shapiro, George Shultz, and I form a regular luncheon group that meets irregularly at George's campus home. In the course of those lunches, many occasions arose to discuss universities.

Regina was the first to read a draft and, of course, participated in innumerable discussions of its subject matter over many decades. Throughout our life together we have agreed not only on the value of universities but, more important, on what universities should value. To her I owe my greatest debt.

The book is dedicated to Katherine and Matthew George, our grandchildren. In secondary school now, they will, in a few years, have the pleasure and responsibility of assuring that studies blossom and minds move.

Index

Academic Bill of Rights, 134, 137–39

Academic Council of the Academic Senate of the University of California, 129

Academic freedom, x, 34, 37, 65, 81, 97, 113, 135–40, 170, 174–75, 184, 186, 194. *See also* Freedoms of and freedoms in the university

Accountability of professors, 175

Accrediting associations, 118–19, 126–33. *See also* Western Association of Schools and Colleges (WASC)

Adler, Mortimer, 48

Admissions policies, 90, 146–52, 154–55. *See also* Affirmative action

Affirmative action: ambivalence on, 154; California Civil Rights Initiative (Proposition 209), 143–44, 152–53; context, 151–54; debate over, 142–43; and equal opportunity, 142; individuality of applicants, 150–51; and integration, 158; and merit, 142, 152, 154; and minority alumni program,

155–59; minority applicants, 147–49; postscripts, 155–67; subtext, 154–55; and tenure decisions, 160–67; text of address (October 4, 1995), 141–51; University of California Regents' resolution to end (1995), 151–52

Agassiz, Louis, 28, 170

Alexander, Lamar, 129–30

Alumni: children of, admissions policy for, 147; minority alumni program, 155–59; relations role of university president, 9–10, 12

American Association of University Professors, 195

"Angry young men" and antiestablishment writers, xvii–xviii

Annual Register: 1895–96, 71; *1899–1900,* 72

Anti-Semitism, 57

Appiah, Kwame Anthony, 100

Arendt, Hannah, xvii, 189–90, 192

Asian-American students and Asian-American studies, 88, 101–2, 105–6, 109

Athletes as applicants, 147

Autonomous individual free to speak and be viewed without regard to labels, 23, 52, 61, 68, 95–96, 101, 112, 151

Baruch College, 130
Beida. *See* Peking University
Beijing University. *See* Peking University
Bellow, Saul, 14, 93
Berger, Karol, 200–201
Berkeley. *See* University of California
Bickel, Alexander, xii, 84
Biddle, Paul, 31
Biehl, Amy, 92
Bing, Peter, 39
Bing Overseas Studies Program, 186
Black, Charles, xii, 84
Bloom, Allan, 30
Borchert, Wolfgang, xviii
Bourne, Randolph, 96
The Brandeis/Frankfurter Connection: The Secret Political Activities of Two Supreme Court Justices (Murphy), 82
Brest, Iris, 76
Brown, Jerry, 153, 198
Budget reductions, 104
Burciaga, Cecilia, 105
Bush, Vannevar, 29, 198

Cai Yuanpei, 170–71
California Civil Rights Initiative (Proposition 209), 143–44, 152–53
California Environmental Protection Agency, 125

Campus Disruption Policy (1967), 74, 76, 124
Campus diversity, 75–76, 87–110; and ambiguous use of terminology, 100; demographic profile of class of *1997,* 88–89; and dynamism of culture, 95; ethnic centers funding, 104; *Final Report of the University Committee on Minority Issues* (1989), 99; and "republic of learning," 96–97; and social/cultural identity, 92–94; and theme residences, 75, 91, 101–2, 105; and university policy, 94–95; vision statement on, 99. *See also* Affirmative action; Multiculturalism
The Care and Culture of Men (Jordan), 72
Cares of the University (Casper), xxii, 11
Carter, Stephen, 62
Casper, Gerhard: background of, xi–xxi, 66; Berkeley faculty position, xx, 123–24; high school education of, xv–xviii; Stanford career after presidency, xxiii; Stanford president, xxi–xxii; university education of, xviii–xix; University of Chicago career, xxi, 124–25, 156; and World War II, xi–xiii; Yale Law School graduate work, xix–xx
Casper, Regina, xiii, 28; married to Gerhard Casper, xx; professor of psychiatry, xx–xxi
Centennial Campaign, 9, 32

Founding Grant (1885), 55, 70,
97, 145, 194
Fourteenth Amendment, 143
Fraga, Luis, 108
Fragility of universities, 36, 106,
112, 125
Frankfurter, Felix: criticism of
political activity of, 82; on essay
as literary form, x; on preventing
intervention in universities,
117–18, 136, 140; in *Sweezy v.
New Hampshire* (1957), 66,
113–14, 136–37; "wise government," principle of, 123
Franklin, Bruce, 74
Freedom from distraction, 175–76,
199
Freedom of association, 66, 73, 80,
81, 91
Freedoms of and freedoms in the
university, x, 22–26, 42–53;
avoiding dominant ways of
thinking, 23, 79; challenging
established orthodoxy, 23, 35;
challenging new orthodoxy, 23,
35, 79, 112–13; conducting
highest-quality research, 25;
effect of information technology
on, 202; engaging in global
contacts, 24–25; and German
model, 170; participating in
public service, 24, 25, 189, 191,
193, 195; pursuit of knowledge,
22, 96, 150, 178; self-
governance and academic
freedom, 113, 119, 121, 135–40,
174–75; speaking as autonomous
individual who is viewed without

regard to labels, 23, 52, 61, 68,
95–96, 112, 151; speaking
plainly, without concealment, and
to the point, 23, 35, 60, 65, 79,
95; student use of campus facilities for protests, 35–36, 106,
123–25; taking pleasure in life of
the mind, 23–24, 42. *See also*
Fundamental Standard; Politics
"Free Expression and Discriminatory Harassment." *See* Fundamental Standard
Freeman Spogli Institute for
International Studies, xxiii
Free speech. *See* First Amendment
rights; Freedoms of and freedoms in the university
Free Speech Movement, 35, 123
Freshman Convocation, 37
Freund, Paul, 24, 37, 84
Fundamental Standard, 64–86;
ambivalence toward Grey
Interpretation, 67–68; chilling
effect of Grey Interpretation, 79;
Grey Interpretation, 31, 35,
64–66, 69, 73, 77, 78, 82; initial
declaration of, 71, 73–74; speech
in violation of, 64, 66; text of,
31, 64
Fund-raising, xxii, 9–10, 32, 155

Galatians, 56, 59, 60
Gay Liberation: vandalism of
sculpture by George Segal, 107
Gender discrimination alleged in
tenure decisions, 160–67
German model of university,
170–73

Germany: postwar, xiv–xviii; World
War II, xi–xiii
Gibbons, James, 174, 183
GI Bill (1944), 126
Globalization, 24–25, 180, 202–3
Goethe, 15–16, 203–4
Golden ages, 43–49
Government-university interac-
tions, 25–26, 114–15, 122,
126–27, 136, 140; state interest
in eradicating discrimination,
65, 66. *See also* Federal research
grants; Regulatory compliance of
higher education
Graduate Fellowships Program,
xxiii
Grapes, university-wide ban on,
105–9
Gray, Hanna, xxi, 27
"Great Books," 48
Gregg, Robert, 60
Grey, Thomas, 69, 74–75, 77
Grey Interpretation. *See* Funda-
mental Standard
Griswold, A. Whitney, 14
Grutter v. Bollinger (2003), 153,
157, 159
Gunther, Gerald, 27, 69, 77, 82;
Casper's remarks at memorial
service for (2002), 82–86

Hamburg in World War II, xi–xiii,
xvi–xvii
Hand, Learned, 82–83
Harassment: motivated by racial or
other bigotry, 65–66, 76; by
personal vilification, 31, 64, 78;
sexual harassment policy, 102;

university's commitment to
prevent hostile environment,
68–69, 77. *See also* Fighting
words; Fundamental Standard
Harding, Warren, 190
Harper, William Rainey, 46
Harvard University presidency, 26
Hate speech. *See* Fighting words;
Fundamental Standard; Harass-
ment
Hazardous waste regulations,
115–17
Hebrew literature, protest against
banning of, 20–21, 22, 57
Hennessy, John, 134, 155, 186,
201–2
Herder, Johann Gottfried,
100–101
Hesiod, 43–44, 47, 51
Hesse, Konrad, xviii–xix
Higher Education Act (1965),
118–19, 122, 127–28
Hill, Thomas, 61
Hockfield, Susan, 193
Holborn, Hajo, 60
Holmes, Justice, 66
Hoover, Herbert, xiii–xiv, 180–81
Horowitz, David, 134
Hostile environment. *See* Fighting
words; Fundamental Standard;
Harassment; Prejudice
Hua Di, 184–87
Humanism, 34
Humboldt, Alexander von, 28, 170
Humboldt, Wilhelm von, 28, 42,
170–75
Humboldtian model of university,
171

Hundred Day Reform of 1898 (China), 170–73
Hunt, Albert R., 3–4
Hutchins, Robert Maynard, ix, 12–13, 46–49
Hutten, Ulrich von, 20–26, 38–40, 55–58, 60–61, 97
"Hutten's Last Days" (Meyer), 21
Huxley, Thomas, 199

Inaugural Address (October 2, 1992): context, 26–37; postscripts, 39–53; subtext, 37–39; text, 17–26
Indirect costs controversy. *See* Research costs, controversy over
Individualism. *See* Autonomous individual free to speak and be viewed without regard to labels
Information technology's effect on universities, 178–80, 201
Innovation, 134, 168, 171, 174, 177, 182, 196–200
Institutional cohesiveness, importance of, 202–4
Integration, 10, 158, 176, 201
Invectives, 55–58, 61
Invectives (Hutten), 21, 55

Jackson, Jesse, 30
James, Henry, 201
Jaspers, Karl, 189, 192
Jefferson, Thomas, 96
Jiang Zemin, 183, 185
Johns Hopkins University, 170
Jordan, David Starr: admissions policy, 146; advice on how to get along with, 22; *The Care and*

Culture of Men address, 72; and Fundamental Standard, 70–72; and German model of university, 170, 171; Hutten and humanism as interests of, 20, 22–23, 26; mentor relationship with Agassiz, 28; and motto, 17–21, 34, 40, 55, 97; and Ross resignation from faculty, 194–95
Judgment without understanding, 58, 61

Kalven, Harry, 13, 25, 36, 109
Karst, Kenneth, 84
Kaufmann, Karl, xiii
Kennedy, David, 11, 199
Kennedy, Donald, 17, 27, 29–33, 77, 155
Kennedy, Randall, 52
Kerr, Clark, 13–14
Knowledge, pursuit of, 22, 96, 150, 172, 178, 191, 197–98, 200
Kurland, Philip, 82, 84, 138

Labor Department, U.S., 160, 162–63
Land use, 4
Lasswell, Harold, xix
Legal issues facing university president, 7–8
Leonard Law (California 1992), 65–67, 69–70, 75, 80–82
Letters of Obscure Men (Hutten), 21
Levi, Edward, xxi, 10, 52–53, 112, 124, 197
Levin, Richard, 192–93
Lewis, John, 185

Lewis, Michael, 200
Lewis, Oscar, 59
Light, Richard J., 121
Livingston, Randall, 41
Loma Prieta earthquake (1989), 29, 32
Lovejoy, Arthur, 135
Lubot, Eugene, 171
Luther, Martin, 21, 23, 55, 83
Lutheran Church–Missouri Synod v. Federal Communications Commission (D.C. Cir. 1998), 167
Lyman, Richard, x, 17, 74, 77, 79, 84, 122, 124

Mahood, Gail, 110
Maintenance of physical plant of university, 8, 104
Mansfield, Harvey, 5
Marx, C. D., 39
Mausoleum for Stanford family, 62–63
McDougal, Myres, xix
McEwen, Arthur, 59
Meyer, Conrad Ferdinand, 21
Micah (Prophet), 56, 60
Minority applicants, 147–48. *See also* Affirmative action
Min Weifang, 183–84, 186
More, Thomas, 21, 23
Motto. *See* Stanford motto
Multiculturalism, 33, 38, 94, 98–101, 143
Multinationals, universities as, 203
Musil, Robert, 200
Myers, Woodrow, 91

National Collegiate Athletic Association (NCAA), 2
Native Americans, 15, 78, 89–90, 101, 109, 147
Nazis, responsibility of German character for, xiv
Neal, Phil, xxi
Neo-Confucian values, 171
The New New Thing (Lewis), 200
Newspaper reporting about universities, 3, 30, 33, 36
New York Times: on Casper's inaugural address, 36; on Casper's Stanford appointment, 33
No Grapes (documentary), 105, 112
Noncommunitarian community, 112
Notre Dame, 3
Nuremberg war crimes trials, xiii
Nussbaum, Martha, 96

O'Connor, Sandra Day, 157, 159
Office for Multicultural Development, 99
Office of Federal Contract Compliance Programs (OFCCP), 160, 162–63
Office of Naval Research (ONR), 31–32
Office of Residential Education, 101
Ogletree, Charles, 155
Online teaching, 179, 201–3
On the Natural History of Destruction (Sebald), xi–xii
"On the Spirit and Organizational Framework of Intellectual Institutions in Berlin" (Humboldt), 171–72

Oppenheimer, Robert, 191
Outsider status, 3, 33–34

Partnership of industry and universities, 176–77
Partnership of students and faculty, xxii–xxiii, 24, 46, 52–53, 174, 180
Paul's letter to the Galatians, 56, 59, 60
Peking University: Bing Overseas Studies Program, 186; centennial of, 12, 182–83; context, 181–86; history of, 169–70, 181–82; Lee Jung Sen building, 187; parallels to Stanford, 170–71, 178, 181; postscript, 186–87; ranking of, 182, 183; relations with in light of arrest of Hua Di, 184–87; Stanford Center at, 186–87; text of address (May 3, 1998), 168–81
Pendergrass, Walter, 97–98
Periclean age, 44
"Persilscheine" (whitewash papers), xiv
Petersen, Rudolf, xiii
Pitzer, Kenneth, 33
Polanyi, Michael, 28
Political correctness, 34, 69
Politics: faculty members' expression of views on, 25, 135, 137, 139, 198–99; university as political actor, 35, 109; university president's expression of views on, 12–13, 25, 198–99; university's freedom from, 174–75, 184, 194, 197

"Politics of recognition," 100
Poorly stated problems, 191
Postwar Germany, xii–xviii
Prejudice, 56–57, 60–62. *See also* Racism
Presidents Work Group, 131
Private universities: and affirmative action, 159–60; and California Proposition 209, 153; right to set educational policies vs. state regulation, 65–67, 69–70, 74–75, 80–81, 115–16, 157
"Procedures and Criteria for Appointment, Reappointment, and Promotion of Faculty in the School of Humanities and Sciences at Stanford" (Wessells), 161
Proposition 209 (California Civil Rights Initiative), 143–44, 152–53
Protestantism, 21, 171
Provost's Committee on the Recruitment and Retention of Women, 103
Public service, 24, 25, 189, 191, 193, 195
Public welfare. *See* Contribution to human welfare as measure of university
Purposes of universities, ix, 10, 22–28, 197–98, 200–201

Quotas, 142, 143, 147, 154

Race. *See* Affirmative action; Campus diversity
Racism, 75–76, 112. *See also* Fighting words; Prejudice

Radcliffe-Brown, Alfred, 93
Ravelstein (Bellow), 14
R.A.V. v. City of St. Paul (1992), 67
"Reasoned engagement," 192–93
Redfield, James, 49–50
Regulatory compliance of higher
  education, 7, 114–15, 126–40.
  See also Private universities
Renaissance humanism, 34, 43
Report on the University's Role in
  Political and Social Action
  (University of Chicago), 13, 25,
  36
"Repositioning and Simplification"
  initiative, 30
"Republic of learning," 96–97, 192
Reputation of institution, 9
Research, regulation of, 26,
  115–16, 160
Research costs, controversy, 31–33,
  37–38
Research funding, 28–29, 197. *See*
  also Federal research grants
Research in conjunction with
  teaching as dual focus of
  university, xii–xiii, 24, 46,
  172–73, 202
Research-intensive university,
  169–87; contribution to human
  welfare, 180–81, 193–94,
  197–98; distinguished from
  research university, 169; freedom
  from distraction in, 175–76,
  199; freedom to set agenda and
  openness to serendipity, 177–78;
  and German model of university,
  170–71; information technology's effect on, 178–80;

partnership of industry with
  university, 176–77; partnership
  of students and faculty in, 174,
  180; self-governance and
  academic freedom in, 174–75;
  size of student body in, 175;
  survival of, 203; teaching and
  research as dual focus of, 24, 46,
  172–73, 202
Rice, Condoleezza, 6–7, 104–6,
  108–9, 160, 162–65, 185
Rockefeller, John D., 46
Role models, xiv–xv, xviii, 50–52
Rosaldo, Renato, 92–93
Rosovsky, Henry, 199
Ross, Edward, 194–95
Ross, John, 15–16

Sahlins, Marshall, 24
Salovey, Peter, 193
Sample, Steven B., 118
San Francisco Examiner on
  Leonard Law, 66
San Jose Mercury News: cartoon of
  university president application
  form, 15; on OFCCP investiga-
  tion of Stanford, 162; Sowell
  column on affirmative action, 153
Savio, Mario, 123
Sawislak, Karen, 160
Saxenian, Annalee, 177
Scalia, Antonin, 67
Schelsky, Helmut, xvii
Schmidt, Benno, 14
Schmidt, Helmut, xv
Schmitt, Carl, 61
Scholar role of university president,
  11

Schwartz, John, 76
Schweitzer, Albert, xvi
"Science, the Endless Frontier"
	(Bush), 29, 198
"Search to know." *See* Knowledge,
	pursuit of
Sebald, W. G., xi–xii
Self-censorship, 34, 60, 79
Self-criticism, 191, 197
Self-examination and self-
	cultivation, 171
Self-regulation of higher education,
	127. *See also* Accrediting
	associations
Sexual harassment policy, 102
Shapiro, Harold, 3
Sheehan, James, 17, 27, 39, 110, 195
Shils, Edward, 175–76, 199
Shoven, John, 109, 160
Silicon Valley, 169, 171, 176–77,
	183, 199, 200
The Skeptical Generation
	(Schelsky), xvii
SLAC National Accelerator
	Laboratory, 5
Smith, Anna Deavere, 149
Social engineering, 95, 101
Social identity, 92–94, 100
Social worker role of university
	president, 13–14
South African divestment, 36
Sowell, Thomas, 153
Speech acts, ix
Spelling, Margaret, 132
Spitz, Lew, 56, 57, 60
Stahl, Erna, xv–xvii
Stanford (Alumni Association
	magazine), 62

Stanford, Jane, 4, 54, 55, 60, 145,
	193–94
Stanford, Leland, 4, 55, 58–59, 70,
	145
Stanford Alumni Association,
	40–41, 62
Stanford Band, 3
Stanford Fund, 155
Stanford Golf Course, 15
Stanford Illustrated Review, on
	Stanford motto, 40
Stanford in Turmoil (Lyman), x
Stanford Management Company, 6
Stanford motto, 17–21, 34, 39–42,
	55, 67, 79, 97, 113
Stanford Report, reprinting of
	speeches in, 62
Stanford Research Park, 176
Stanford Review caricature of
	Native American (1994), 78
Stanford seal, 17, 39–42, 97. *See
	also* Stanford motto
Stanford's history, 28–29, 169–70,
	193–94. *See also* Stanford, Jane;
	Stanford, Leland
"Statement on Diversity" (Western
	Association of Schools and
	Colleges), 103–4, 128–29
State of the University Address
	(May 12, 1994): context, 123–31;
	postscripts, 131–40; text, 111–23
State Postsecondary Review
	Entities (SPREs), 118–19,
	131–32
Steinbeck, John, 13
Steiner, George, 47
Stereotyping, 60–61. *See also*
	Prejudice; Racism

Sterling, Wallace, 18–19, 28
Stigler, George, 50, 138, 139–40
Stigler, Stephen, 202
Stone, Peter, 70, 77, 80
Strauss, David Friedrich, 20, 21
Strober, Myra, 103
Student Conduct Legislative
  Council, 31, 64, 67, 76, 77
Student loan programs, adminis-
  tration of, 118–19, 126–27
Student speech: campus facilities
  used in student protests, 35–36,
  74, 124; right to challenge
  faculty on academic grounds, 37;
  students learning from students,
  50, 52. *See also* Autonomous
  individual free to speak and be
  viewed without regard to labels;
  Fundamental Standard
Sunday Night Flicks, 105, 112
Sweezy v. New Hampshire (1957),
  66–67, 113–14, 136–37

Taube Center for Jewish Studies,
  109
Taylor, Charles, 92, 100
Teaching and research as dual
  focus of university, 46, 172–73,
  202
Technology transfer, 174, 176, 201
Tenure decisions, 160–67
Terman, Fred, 28
Terman, Lewis, 146
Theme residences, 75, 91, 101–2,
  105
A Theory of Art (Berger), 200–201
Thielicke, Helmut, xviii
Transience, dangers of, 200

Tremaine, Frank, 38
Trow, Martin, 129
Trustee role of university president,
  8–9
Truth, 200

Ujamaa (African-American theme
  house) incident (1988), 75–76
Undergraduate general education
  requirements, 193
United Farm Workers of America,
  108
Unity within the university, 38
University of Berlin, 172
University of California: Academic
  Council of the Academic Senate,
  129; Berkeley, xx, 35, 123–24;
  Regents' resolution to end
  affirmative action (1995),
  151–52
University of Chicago: Aims of
  Education Address (1990), 43;
  "Battle of Chicago," 47–48;
  Casper at, xx–xxi, 156; founding
  of, 170; Hutchins's curriculum,
  46–49; *Report on the University's
  Role in Political and Social
  Action*, 13, 25, 36; student
  protests, 124–25; teaching and
  research as dual focus of, 46,
  197
University of Michigan Law School
  case (*Grutter v. Bollinger* (2003),
  153, 157, 159
"The University of the Twenty-First
  Century" (conference 1998), 183
University president, 1–16; alumni
  relations role of, 9–10; as CEO,